T0169647

REACHING THE FINISH LINE

"*Reaching The Finish Line* is a must read for anyone who is looking to discover the champion inside them. Kallen truly delivers in this inspirational and practical guide to success."

—**Bethany Marshall**, The Ultimate Fighter

"If you are unemployed, underemployed or just simply hate your job, Kallen will teach you how to Reach the Finish Line!"

—**Gordon D'Angelo**, Founder of Jackson Hewitt
& NY Times Bestselling Author

"Kudos to Kallen for putting together such a wonderful resource. Read this book to learn how to get a great career despite your educational background and most importantly how to get your mental fitness in order. His keen insight and dedication to articulate such a powerful message is priceless."

—**Ben Fuchs**, The Anti-Drug Pharmacist &
Host of the Nationally Syndicated Radio Show: The Bright Side

REACHING THE
FINISH LINE

*A Practical Guide
to Discovering the*
CHAMPION
IN YOU

KALLEN DIGGS

NEW YORK

REACHING THE FINISH LINE
A Practical Guide to Discovering the CHAMPION IN YOU

© 2015 **KALLEN DIGGS**.

All rights reserved. No portion of this book may be reproduced, stored in a retrieval system, or transmitted in any form or by any means—electronic, mechanical, photocopy, recording, scanning, or other,—except for brief quotations in critical reviews or articles, without the prior written permission of the publisher.

Published in New York, New York, by Morgan James Publishing. Morgan James and The Entrepreneurial Publisher are trademarks of Morgan James, LLC. www.MorganJamesPublishing.com

The Morgan James Speakers Group can bring authors to your live event. For more information or to book an event visit The Morgan James Speakers Group at www.TheMorganJamesSpeakersGroup.com.

A **free** eBook edition is available
with the purchase of this print book.

CLEARLY PRINT YOUR NAME ABOVE IN UPPER CASE

Instructions to claim your free eBook edition:
1. Download the BitLit app for Android or iOS
2. Write your name in **UPPER CASE** on the line
3. Use the BitLit app to submit a photo
4. Download your eBook to any device

ISBN 978-1-63047-378-5 paperback
ISBN 978-1-63047-379-2 eBook
ISBN 978-1-63047-380-8 hardcover
Library of Congress Control Number:
2014946496

Cover Design by:
Rachel Lopez
www.r2cdesign.com

Interior Design by:
Bonnie Bushman
bonnie@caboodlegraphics.com

In an effort to support local communities, raise awareness and funds, Morgan James Publishing donates a percentage of all book sales for the life of each book to Habitat for Humanity Peninsula and Greater Williamsburg.

Get involved today, visit
www.MorganJamesBuilds.com

Habitat
for Humanity®
Peninsula and
Greater Williamsburg
Building Partner

Table of Contents

Are You Ready?

Are you ready? No, I don't mean if you are ready to read this book. Let me clarify. Are you ready to achieve your goal? A lot of people claim that they want to achieve certain things in their life. However, if you look at their lifestyle, it is not a reflection of what they really want in their life.

We all know the people that say that they want to make more money. They appear me to be convincing. However, once we take a closer look at their lifestyle, we learn that they haven't done anything to increase their financial income. I'm surprised these people aren't annoyed with themselves. Sometimes, people don't have any intention of increasing their financial income but rather to say things to please people.

I believe there are people who are ready to do what's necessary to achieve their goal, even if they don't have a sense of direction. It is this attitude that propels people to success fairly quickly. Martin Luther King said it best, "Take the first step. You don't have to see the whole staircase.

Just take the first step." Unless you are fortunate enough to come from a wealthy family or from a family that is well connected, you will soon realize that everything is not going to be drawn out for you. That's why you need to begin. The details will come later. Jack Canfield illustrates it by saying, "Think of this: a car driving through the night. The headlights only go 100 to 200 feet forward. And you can make it all the way from California to New York driving through the dark because all you have to see is the next 200 feet. And that's how life tends to unfold for us."

We are fortunate to live in today's world where information can be easily accessed through the internet. The internet puts us at a great advantage today than our ancestors 100 years ago. You don't need someone to hold your hand. It is easy enough to figure out. The abundance of information provided on the internet dramatically reduces the learning curve for anyone.

There is a truth that some people are afraid to blindly immerse themselves in any new pursuit. Some people want to know everything before they start something. The reality is those people will never start because everything will not be laid out. This is a normal occurrence in any situation. Let's apply it to dating: you are not going to know everything about your date prior to dating. Let's apply it to a job: you are not going to know everything about the employer prior to applying for the position. This is a universal fact.

So, let's revisit the original question. Are you ready? Let's go through a checklist to determine if you're really ready.

Are you spending time with the wrong people?

Are you trying to be someone that you're not?

Are you scared of making mistakes?

Are you wasting your time trying to gain approval from others?

Are you lacking self-confidence?

If you were able to answer NO to all 5 questions, then skip to the next page. If you weren't able to answer NO to all 5 questions, then you have a problem. This problem is the very thing that is stopping you from succeeding.

If you are spending time with the wrong people, then you need to stop spending time with them. Instead, start spending time with people that support your goals.

If you are trying to be someone that you're not, you need to stop and question your motives. Why not become someone that you will be proud of? Isn't that the whole point of living?

If you are scared of making mistakes, you need to accept that mistakes are part of the learning process. Even the most successful people have risen from suffering the consequences of their bad mistakes.

If you are wasting your time trying to gain approval from others, then you need to stop. Start living the life the way you intended, not the way others intended. After all, you are the creator of your own destiny. Do you really want someone else to be in charge of it?

If you are not confident in yourself, then you need to learn to be more confident in yourself. Reflect back on your past successes and use those experiences as your foundation. Henry Ford said it best: "Whether you think you can or think you can't, either way you're right." It's the mind that makes it so.

If you were able to answer NO to all 5 questions, then you are ready to move forward. You are truly ready to begin your quest.

When you surround yourself with a supportive group, you feel encouraged and motivated to proceed.

When you are true to whom you are, you are much happier and more excited about the possibilities that you can have in your life.

When you are not scared of making mistakes, you become fearless in taking risks and wiser from every experience.

When you stop wasting your time trying to gain approval from others, you begin to live your life the way you intended. You realize that you have control of your destiny which influences you to take a proactive role in your life.

When you are confident in yourself, you influence others to be confident in you. When others are confident in you, you become more confident in yourself. It's the "dog chasing his tail" effect.

This book is applicable to anyone inspired to pursue their financial and/or career goals. If you were ever a high school student, then this book is definitely for you.

To get the greatest benefit from this book, my advice is for you to read through the book the first time and then read the book for the second time as you make progress towards your goal. Sow a seed in someone's life by sharing this book with someone you care about. I'm almost certain that they will appreciate it.

I believe in you. I also believe that we are born here with the tools needed to be successful. No one is deprived. We all share one thing and that is our will. Your will determines whether you will succeed or fail. I am happy for you and strongly feel that this book will make the difference in your life.

Are you ready for the race of your life?

CHAPTER 1

Ready for the Race of Your Life

The race of your life is like a marathon. Everyone has a different reason for running it. Some people may run it for health related reasons while others may run it to be a part of a cause. The same applies to our goals. We are all working towards something for a particular reason. What is the real motive behind your ambition?

You might be someone who comes from a poor neighborhood. So, your goal may be attaining financial stability in which your motive could be creating financial security for you and/or your parent(s).

You might be someone who was abused as a child and been told that you will always be a failure. Perhaps, you've believed it for a while. Your goal is to prove yourself and the other doubters wrong by working towards the goal that is going to complete you and make you feel ecstatic about life.

You might be someone who has a physical or mental disability. Your goal may be to prove to yourself and the doubters that you are capable of achieving whatever your heart desires.

You might be someone who hates their job. So, your goal may be to find a career that coincides with your passion, which will satisfy you personally and professionally.

You might be someone who hates working for someone else. So, your goal may be to start your own business or find a profession that allows you to be your own boss.

These are only a few of many examples that may relate to a person's situation. Everyone has a motive. When there is a motive, the next to come is the motivation. The motive and motivation cannot be separated. They are dependent upon each other. You cannot have motivation with no motive or a motive with no motivation.

Perhaps, you may think that the words motive and motivation are interchangeable. It is true that the two words can be used synonymously in some cases. However, there is a difference that many people aren't aware of. Motive is the specific reason for performing a specific action. Motivation is the feeling that makes you want to perform the specific action.

Do you see the difference? If not, let's zoom in on it. The motive is the reason of why you're doing it and the motivation is the feeling that is driving you to do it. In the following examples, notice how each motive describes the reason for the aspiration while each motivation uses words of emotion to describe the necessity for pursuing that goal.

Motive: I want a job that allows me to use my creativity because it can help improve a company's sales.

Motivation: I'm tired of working a job that limits possibilities and restricts my ability to be creative.

Motive: I want to go to a college that pays for my tuition. A tuition-free education will eliminate my risk of going into debt.

Motivation: I hate spending thousands of dollars at a college, especially in this economy. I can't afford to graduate with 50 thousand dollars in student loans and a strong likelihood of not finding a great career.

Motive: I want to be self-employed because I prefer to create my own schedule and make my own decisions.

Motivation: I do not like working long hours and working on the weekends.

You should now have a better idea of distinguishing the motive and the motivation. What is your motive? What is your motivation? The answers to these questions are the prerequisite to running the race of your life. Without those answers, you will be like a person trying to guess their way from Los Angeles to New York City instead of having a roadmap or GPS.

Most of us obtain driving directions in one of 3 ways: print out instructions (via Google Maps, Mapquest, etc), a GPS monitor, or a roadmap. You can say that a roadmap is akin to a blog. Blogs are known for their concentrated information on a certain topic. Print out instructions is akin to having a book. Like a book, you have to read the instructions to know how to proceed successfully. You can say that a GPS is akin to having a mentor. Like a GPS, a mentor is there to provide you with step by step instructions and ongoing support to assure that you stay on the right path.

Believe it or not, following instructions can be difficult for some people. The fact of the matter is that it sounds easy but it is not always easy. Some people are too stubborn to do what they are told even if it will make them successful. As humans, we have a tendency to take ideas and analyze them through our scope of reasoning. The ideas that we are presented may make us doubtful despite its effectiveness. Some people will say that it doesn't make sense to me so I'm not going to do it. There is no wonder why they are not successful.

I am not suggesting that you should throw your brain out of the window and do everything you're told. However, I am suggesting that you take advice from successful people regarding your pursuits. Successful people know what works and they continue to be successful because they apply methods that work. Whether you're reading their blog, their book, or a member of their seminar or coaching program, follow their instructions exactly. Don't try to slightly modify instructions based on what you think will work. FOLLOW INSTRUCTIONS!

Your goal may seem like a long and challenging journey. The truth is that some of us don't want to take the long road. We live in a society that promotes instant gratification. We live in an era where everything is about convenience. A lot of people will opt out from doing things because it is not convenient for them. These are the same type of people who would rather play the lottery because it is fast and convenient. You are welcome to play the lottery for the rest of your life, hoping for instant gratification. Be sure to send me an email to let me know how much money you're making from the lottery.

All of this ever growing state of convenience is reducing people's work ethic, which in turn makes people lazier. Convenience is not always bad though. Sometimes, it can increase productivity in various situations. The smartphone is one example. It has made email, GPS, and other apps more accessible when we're on the go. So, convenience is more of a neutral agent that can be helpful or abused based on the person's intent. If you are going to use any type of technology or other resource to make your life convenient, ask yourself if it is making you more productive.

In order for you to be successful, you must learn discipline. I know that's not what a lot of you want to hear but it's the hard reality that we need to accept in our lives. It is the primary trait that successful people possess. If you have ever been in the military, then you should know discipline better than anyone else. Discipline is the tool that helps us stay on course. It helps you avoid procrastinating, acting on impulse, and breaking promises that you made to yourself or others.

No one out there is going to discipline you. You are the founder and owner of (Your Name) Life INC. You need to employ self-discipline if you intend to see any good results. Self-discipline is one's ability to be able to behave in a strict and controlled manner. Now, it may sound like doom and gloom to some of you. However, in reality, self-discipline yields a lot of freedom. Let's say that you commit yourself in applying for one virtual position daily. Once you get hired and start working from home full time, you can plan to travel more. You could visit a city or relocate to a city as often as you like. Wouldn't it be great to have that freedom?

I bet that you have several routine habits that you aren't willing to give up. What would you sacrifice if you knew that you would be successful? A lot of people would say that they would sacrifice it all. However, a lot of those people are saying that with the assumption that they will be successful immediately as soon as they sacrifice everything. Those people are thinking unrealistically.

The next thing that you will need is patience. Once you vowed to discipline yourself, you are going to need patience to sustain your efforts. Michael Jordan didn't become the best basketball player by scoring 16 points in his first game. Patience was required from him to become one of the greatest basketball players. Do you have the patience that is required to be successful?

Everybody lacks patience. Don't be deceived in thinking somebody has an unlimited supply of patience. We are all impatient about something. In our lives, there are areas in where we are more patient as well as areas where we aren't so patient. A simple way to be more patient is by being more realistic about things. So many people are disappointed with themselves because of their unrealistic expectations.

The last thing that you will need is happiness. A lot of people will say that I will be happy once I am successful. While that is certainly true for most people, it is important to enjoy the process along the way. Happiness builds momentum. If you are not happy about your journey to success, then you are likely to fail.

Ask yourself these following questions:

Are you enjoying the journey from where you are to where you want to be?

Are you enjoying the journey even though you haven't reached your destination yet?

If you answered no to at least one of the questions, then perhaps it may be worth revisiting your motives for wanting to achieve whatever you desire. My suspicions would say that your attitude may be what is hindering yourself from enjoying the journey. Your attitude forms every situation in your life, whether you are aware of it or not. It is constantly challenged by people and external factors. Will you control your attitude?

There is an infectious and negative attitude that prompts people to say things like "I'll believe it when I see it." The problem with this statement is that most people never get started. They are too lazy to give it a try. The fact of the matter is some people have already been successful which shows the evidence that it works. The bottom line is some people are determined to be successful and some people aren't as determined. It's all in your attitude. Which side of the fence are you on?

The worst thing that you can do is to tell yourself that you will wait until New Years to commit a goal. Make the commitment to start today. Why wait days, weeks, or months for New Years to begin? More than half of people that set New Year's resolutions fail. Think about that for a moment. People waste all of their time from that point until New Years waiting to start a resolution only to fail weeks or months later. Why waste precious time that you can never get back? A lot of people say,

"Time is money." That statement is only a half truth. The full truth is that time is limited and can be only wasted or invested. Time is precious which explains why people charge others for their time.

CHAPTER 2

Take the First Step

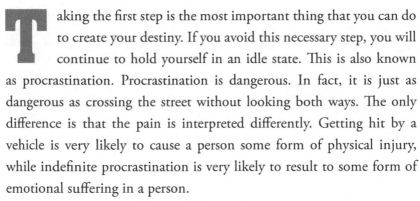

Taking the first step is the most important thing that you can do to create your destiny. If you avoid this necessary step, you will continue to hold yourself in an idle state. This is also known as procrastination. Procrastination is dangerous. In fact, it is just as dangerous as crossing the street without looking both ways. The only difference is that the pain is interpreted differently. Getting hit by a vehicle is very likely to cause a person some form of physical injury, while indefinite procrastination is very likely to result to some form of emotional suffering in a person.

This pain can start compounding if a person continues to ignore their goals. It is by far the worse when a person waits until their senior years to realize that procrastination has gotten the best of them. The truth of the matter is that your age is never a factor because you can always start over by making that choice. You are welcome to allow something like old age to hinder you. However, keep in mind that Colonel Sanders was 65 years old when KFC became a profitable business.

Have you ever pondered on a business idea to find out later that someone took that very idea and made millions with it? How does that make you feel? How does it make you feel when you hesitated to buy real estate at an all-time low but now that real estate is selling for 3 to 4 times as much?

Procrastination is the barrier that separates you from great opportunities. The most common procrastination alibi is "I'll do it later." People don't realize that procrastination labels the word "later" as indefinite. It can be a bad habit to develop because it gives room for distractions, which usually makes people forget about their initial goals.

The most successful people rarely procrastinate, which may explain why they are so successful. However, some people will argue that procrastination is not always bad. The Stanford philosopher, John Perry has been a promoter of the "structured procrastination", a concept that he coined 17 years ago. He disagrees with the old idea that procrastinators should limit their commitments and argues that the key to productivity is to make more commitments but to be methodical about it.

He recommends putting a couple of daunting tasks that are vaguely important and seem to have deadlines at the top of your to-do list. Then, farther down the list, include some doable tasks that really matter. He states that "doing those tasks becomes a way of not doing things higher up on the list. With this sort of appropriate task structure, the procrastinator becomes a useful citizen. Indeed, the procrastinator can even acquire, as I have, a reputation for getting a lot done. The secret to my incredible energy and efficiency in getting work done is a simple one. The psychological principle is this: anyone can do any amount of work, provided it isn't the work he is supposed to be doing at the moment."

University of Calgary psychologist, Piers Steel refers to it as productive procrastination. He argues that "procrastination can be beaten down, but not entirely beaten" and recommends to "play projects off against each other, procrastinating on one by working on another."

In the course of his career, Dr. Steel has surveyed more than 24,000 people around the world and found that 95% of them confess to some form of procrastination. About 25% of them identify themselves as chronic procrastinators. So, as you see, this is a problem that affects just about everyone. So, there is no reason to be hard on yourself. However, when taking the first step to your goal, you need to strategize a plan on how you will deal with procrastination.

While I would subscribe to the traditional way of dealing with procrastination, Dr. Perry and Dr. Steel have offered some great alternatives. Different methods work for different people. I prefer to tackle it by getting whatever needs to be done as soon as possible. If you give yourself enough time, then you can make good progress in achieving your goal in a timely manner. I talk about the importance of self-discipline in the last chapter. Without self-discipline, you will be subjected to procrastination. Time is a friend to no man. You can either move with it or watch it pass by you.

So, how can a person optimize their time? A person will be successful when they learn how to set goals efficiently. The wrong way to write a goal is what Raymond Aaron calls The Dreaded Binary Technique. It looks like this: "I will be the top salesman in the company this month." Then, a person would go on and judge their progress based on a pass or fail basis. If you are successful, you feel good. If you are unsuccessful, you feel bad. Why should you structure goals that give you a probability of failure and feeling bad?

Raymond Aaron invented a proven technique called The MTO Technique. Instead of writing a goal using The Dreaded Binary Technique, you break every goal in 3 levels (minimum, target, outrageous). He defines the minimum as the very least that you can achieve based on your past performance. He defines the target as the stretch or what is slightly beyond the minimum. And lastly, he defines outrageous as the level that you don't believe that you can achieve.

So, let's look at this illustrative example. Janet lives in southern California and works as a distributor for a nutritional supplement company. They give her a 50% profit for any of their products sold on her online store. She wants to get out of debt in 3 years. She knows that she can make $1000 in sales within 1 week because she has done it every week in the past 3 months. So, Janet would set that bar as her minimum goal. Her target goal may be $1500 in sales within 1 week. She feels that is a realistic target. But she would surely be blown away if she did $2000 in sales within 1 week. That would be what she would consider an outrageous goal.

As shown in the example, this approach to setting goals will ensure that you are successful. This is the failproof way to setting goals. Employing the MTO technique as well as avoiding procrastination is my recommended formula for anyone ready to take the first step. All you need to do is take the first step and the next step will be waiting for you.

CHAPTER 3

Land a Career without a High School Diploma

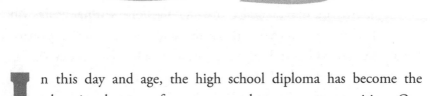

In this day and age, the high school diploma has become the educational norm for most employment opportunities. Our parents always told us to graduate from high school so we can get a good job. There is some truth to that statement. It is definitely not easy to find a great job without a high school diploma. I believe that most high school dropouts had good intentions for not finishing. Perhaps, it wasn't the wisest decision but it was the most appropriate for them at that time.

There are lots of reasons why teenagers drop out of high school. Sometimes, it is attributed to poverty. Sometimes, it is attributed to an unstable household (a parent that is abusive, incarcerated, or dead). Other reasons may be academic difficulties, mental health issues, drug problems, sexual orientation, teenage pregnancy, obesity, or just being bullied in general.

The Gates Foundation did a report (titled "The Silent Epidemic") on this very issue and found some interesting statistics.

- 47% of dropouts stated that not having a diploma makes it hard to find a good job.
- 42% of dropouts spent time with people who were not interested in school.
- 35% of dropouts said that failing in school was the major reason.
- 26% of dropouts said they had become a parent.
- 22% of dropouts said they had to get care for a family member.
- 69% of dropouts stated that they weren't motivated.

Let's take a deeper look into the first statistic. So, only 47% of dropouts stated that they are having trouble. What about the other 53%? This statistic proves that there is hope for high school dropouts. While it surely helps to have a high school diploma, it doesn't dispel doom on a person who doesn't have one. There are other industries that would surely consider a high school dropout if he or she has the experience and/or a great skill set.

So, let's take a look at the professions that don't require a high school diploma. Almost all of these professions require you to be in good physical condition to be considered for the position.

Carpet Installers:

A carpet installer is a person who measures, installs, and cuts carpets and rugs. This person has knowledge of commonly used concepts, practices and procedures within the field. A carpet installer relies on instructions and pre-established guidelines to perform the functions of the job. Their primary job functions do not typically require exercising independent judgment. However, it is necessary that they possess customer service skills, math skills, physical strength, and stamina to be effective at their position. They typically work under supervision and report to a supervisor or manager.

There is no formal education requirement for carpet installers but high school courses in basic math are considered helpful. Most carpet installers learn by helping more experienced workers and gradually getting more duties. Employers provide this training on the job. New carpet installers start by helping to move carpet, after which they progress to cutting and trimming carpet.

National Estimates:

Minimum annual salary:	$21,350
Average annual salary:	$40,930
Maximum annual salary:	$69,530

The 2 industries that have the highest levels of employment in this profession are home furnishing stores and building finishing contractors. Home furnishing stores pay carpet installers an average hourly wage of $18.88 an hour. Building finishing contractors pay carpet installers an average hourly wage of $20.26 an hour.

The following are the top paying industries for this profession:

Industry Hourly mean wage

Traveler accommodation	$25.05
Local Government (OES Designation)	$23.12
Employment Services	$21.73
Elementary and Secondary Schools	$21.51
Nonresidential Building Construction	$20.85

States with the most employed carpet installers:
1. California
2. Illinois
3. Pennsylvania
4. New York
5. Ohio

Top paying states for this profession:
1. Illinois
2. New Jersey
3. Missouri
4. Arizona
5. Minnesota

Drywall Installers:

A drywall installer is a person who plans, installs, and repairs drywalls to cover walls, ceilings, shafts, and movable partitions in residential and commercial structures. This person needs to be familiar with standard concepts, practices, and procedures within the field. A certain level of creativity and latitude is required. It is necessary for drywall installers to possess math skills, physical strength, and stamina to be effective at their position. A drywall installer usually works under general supervision and reports to a supervisor or manager.

There is no formal education requirement for drywall installers but high school math and general shop courses are considered useful. Most drywall installers learn their trade informally by helping more experienced workers and gradually being given more duties. An apprenticeship may not be required if the person has sufficient experience (1-3 years) in the field or a related field.

National Estimates:

Minimum annual salary:	$24,720
Average annual salary:	$42,380
Maximum annual salary:	$72,500

The 2 industries that have the highest levels of employment in this profession are nonresidential building construction and building finishing contractors. Nonresidential building construction companies pay carpet installers an average hourly wage of $22.14 an hour. Building finishing contractors pay carpet installers an average hourly wage of $20.51 an hour.

The following are the top paying industries for this profession:

Industry Hourly mean wage

Other Specialty Trade Contractors	$22.46
Nonresidential Building Construction	$22.14
Building Finishing Contractors	$20.51
Higher Education Institutions	$20.06
Residential Building Construction	$18.40

States with the most employed drywall installers:
1. California
2. Texas
3. Florida
4. New York
5. Virginia

Top paying states for this profession:
1. California
2. Missouri
3. Massachusetts

4. New Jersey
5. Hawaii

Cement Masons/Concrete Finishers:

Cement masons and concrete finishers place and finish concrete. They may color concrete surfaces, expose aggregate (small stones) in walls and sidewalks, or make concrete beams, columns, and panels. It is necessary that cement masons and concrete finishers possess physical strength and stamina to be effective at their position.

Cement masons doing decorative finished work employ design, color, and visual skills. Cement masons tend to work with finished cement forms and mortar to erect walls and other above-ground structures. Cement masons need to be able to follow detailed directions to make complex building components.

Concrete finishers must know how to work quickly and effectively to pour and shape concrete. Concrete finishers pour wet cement into various forms and tend to work on foundation slabs, sidewalks, roads, curbs, and other ground-level projects.

There are no specific education requirements for cement masons and concrete finishers but high school courses in math, mechanical drawing, and blueprint reading are considered to be helpful. Some contractors have their own cement masonry or terrazzo training programs. Although workers may enter apprenticeships directly, many start out as helpers or construction laborers.

National Estimates:

Minimum annual salary:	$23,380
Average annual salary:	$39,870
Maximum annual salary:	$64,080

The 3 industries that have the highest levels of employment in this profession are foundation, structure, and building exterior contractors, other specialty trade contractors and highway, street, and bridge construction.

Foundation, structure, and building exterior contractors pay cement masons/concrete finishers an average hourly wage of $18.42 an hour. Other specialty trade contractors pay cement masons/concrete finishers an average hourly wage of $19.36 an hour. Highway, street, and bridge construction contractors pay cement masons/concrete finishers an average hourly wage of $21.16 an hour.

The following are the top paying industries for this profession:

Industry Hourly mean wage

Industry	Hourly mean wage
General Medical and Surgical Hospitals	$28.14
Architectural and Engineering	$26.67
Management of Companies and Enterprises	$26.39
Federal Executive Branch	$23.20
Local Government (OES Designation)	$22.68

States with the most employed cement masons/concrete finishers:
1. Texas
2. California
3. Florida
4. Illinois
5. Pennsylvania

Top paying states for this profession:
1. Alaska
2. Hawaii
3. New York

4. Illinois

5. New Jersey

Roofers:

A roofer is a person who repair and install the roofs of buildings using a variety of materials, including shingles, asphalt, and metal. This person must be familiar with standard concepts, practices, and procedures within the field. It is necessary for operators to possess balance, physical strength, stamina, and unafraid of heights to be effective at their position. A roofer typically works under general supervision and reports to a supervisor or manager.

There are no formal education requirements for roofers but high school courses in math, shop, mechanical drawing, and blueprint reading are helpful. Most on-the-job training programs consist of informal instruction in which experienced workers teach new workers how to use roofing tools, equipment, machines, and materials.

Some roofers learn through a 3-year apprenticeship. For each year of the program, apprentices must have at least 144 hours of related technical training and 2,000 hours of paid on-the-job training. After completing an apprenticeship program, roofers are considered journey workers who can do tasks on their own.

National Estimates:

Minimum annual salary:	$22,350
Average annual salary:	$38,760
Maximum annual salary:	$60,350

The industry that has the highest levels of employment in this profession is foundation, structure, and building exterior contractors. Foundation, structure, and building exterior contractors pay roofers an average hourly wage of $18.53 an hour.

The following are the top paying industries for this profession:

Industry Hourly mean wage	
Lumber and Other Material Wholesalers	$29.51
State Government (OES Designation)	$27.84
Federal Executive Branch	$27.04
Local Government (OES Designation)	$25.35
Nonresidential Building Construction	$22.79

States with the most employed cement masons/concrete finishers:
1. California
2. Florida
3. Ohio
4. Texas
5. Illinois

Top paying states for this profession:
1. Alaska
2. Connecticut
3. Massachusetts
4. New Jersey
5. Hawaii

Crane/Tower Operators:

A crane/tower operator uses tower and cable equipment to lift and move materials, machinery, or other heavy objects. Operators extend and retract horizontal arms and lower and raise hooks attached to cables at the end of their crane or tower. Operators are usually guided by other workers on the ground using hand signals or a radio. It is necessary for operators to possess alertness, manual dexterity, mechanical and visual ability to be effective at their position. Most crane and tower operators work at construction sites or major ports, where they load and unload cargo. Some also work iron and steel mills.

Although it is not usually required, some companies prefer operators with a high school diploma. Most operators are trained on the job in less than a month. The International Union of Engineers offers apprenticeship programs for operators. Their apprenticeships offer paid on-the-job training with technical instruction.

Several states and many cities require crane operators to be licensed. To get licensed, operators typically must pass a written exam on safety rules and procedures and a skills test to prove that they can control a crane. Crane and tower operators usually have several years of experience in related occupations. They may start as construction laborers and work as construction equipment operators or hoist and winch operators.

National Estimates:

Minimum annual salary:	$29,200
Average annual salary:	$50,610
Maximum annual salary:	$78,870

The 3 industries that have the highest levels of employment in this profession are iron and steel mills and ferroalloy manufacturing, support activities for water transportation, and other specialty trade contractors. Iron and steel mill manufacturers pay their operators an average hourly wage of $21.06 an hour. Other specialty trade contractors pay their operators an average hourly wage of $28.57 an hour. Water transportation companies pay their operators an average hourly wage of $32.51 an hour.

The following are the top paying industries for this profession:

Industry Hourly mean wage

Support activities for water transportation	$32.51
Machinery equipment and supply merchants	$32.18
Natural Gas Distribution	$32.14
Heavy and Civil Engineering Construction	$29.90
Aerospace Parts and Product Manufacturing	$29.37

States with the most employed crane/tower operators:
1. Texas
2. Louisiana
3. California
4. Indiana
5. Ohio

Top paying states for this profession:
1. Alaska
2. Washington
3. Nevada
4. Hawaii
5. Illinois

Loading machine operator:

A loading machine operator loads coal, ore, and other rocks onto shuttles, mine cars, or conveyors for transport from a mine to the surface. These workers generally work underground in mines. They may use power shovels, hoisting engines equipped with scrapers or scoops, and automatic gathering arms that move materials onto a conveyor. It is necessary for operators to possess alertness, manual dexterity, mechanical and visual ability to be effective at their position.

Although it is not usually required, some companies prefer operators with a high school diploma. Most operators are trained on the job in less than a month. The International Union of Engineers offers apprenticeship programs for operators. Their apprenticeships offer paid on-the-job training with technical instruction.

National Estimates:

Minimum annual salary:	$34,710
Average annual salary:	$48,060
Maximum annual salary:	$60,500

The industry that has the highest levels of employment in this profession is coal mining. Coal mining companies pay their operators an average hourly wage of $23.52 an hour.

The following are the top paying industries for this profession:

Industry Hourly mean wage

Support Activities for Mining	$25.19
Metal Ore Mining	$23.81
Coal Mining	$23.52
Nonmetallic Mineral Mining and Quarrying	$17.43
Employment Services	$16.76

States with the most employed loading machine operators:
1. Kentucky
2. West Virginia
3. Illinois
4. Montana
5. Pennsylvania

Top paying states for this profession:
1. West Virginia
2. Utah

3. Montana
4. Pennsylvania
5. New Mexico

Gas compressor/Gas pump station operator:

A gas compressor operator often assists gas treaters and gas pumping station operators while a gas pumping station operator tend compressors that raise the pressure of gas to send it through pipelines. It is necessary that operators possess depth perception, good eye to hand coordination, interpersonal skills, physical strength, and being detail oriented in order to be effective at this position.

The typical level of education required for entry into gas occupations is less than a high school diploma. However, some employers prefer to hire graduates of high school vocational programs in which students learn such skills as basic mechanics, welding, and heavy equipment operations. Most workers start as helpers to experienced workers and learn skills on the job.

National Estimates:

Minimum annual salary:	$33,170
Average annual salary:	$51,840
Maximum annual salary:	$72,110

The industry that has the highest levels of employment in this profession is pipeline transportation of natural gas. Pipeline transport companies pay their operators an average hourly wage of $27.07 an hour.

The following are the top paying industries for this profession:

Industry Hourly mean wage

Natural Gas Distribution	$29.48
Other Pipeline Transportation	$27.17

Pipeline Transportation of Natural Gas	$27.07
Oil and Gas Extraction	$24.58
Management of Companies and Enterprises	$20.54

States with the most employed gas operators:
1. Pennsylvania
2. New Mexico
3. Texas
4. West Virginia
5. Oklahoma

Top paying states for this profession:
1. California
2. New Mexico
3. Arkansas
4. Ohio
5. Wyoming

Rotary drill operator:

A rotary drill operator works mostly in the oil fields and is mostly involved in gas processing. This person carries out the plans for drilling that petroleum engineers have designed by operating equipment that drills the well through the soil and rock formation. Rotary drill operators oversee maintenance of the drill rig, train crews, and observe gauges. They use special tools to locate and recover lost or broken bits, casings, and drill pipes from wells. It is necessary that operators possess depth perception, good eye to hand coordination, interpersonal skills, physical strength, and being detail oriented in order to be effective at this position.

The typical level of education required for entry into oil and gas occupations is less than a high school diploma. However, some employers prefer to hire graduates of high school vocational programs in which students learn such skills as basic mechanics, welding, and heavy equipment operations. Most workers start as helpers to experienced workers and learn skills on the job.

National Estimates:

Minimum annual salary:	$30,990
Average annual salary:	$56,540
Maximum annual salary:	$84,390

The 2 industries that have the highest levels of employment in this profession are support activities for mining and oil and gas extraction. Mining support companies pay their operators an average of hourly wage of $27.08 an hour. Oil and gas extractors pay their operators an average of hourly wage of $27.69 an hour.

The following are the top paying industries for this profession:

Industry Hourly mean wage

Petroleum and Coal Products Manufacturers	$34.39
Oil and Gas Extraction	$27.69
Utility System Construction	$27.38
Support Activities for Mining	$27.08
Other Specialty Trade Contractors	$21.26

States with the most employed rotary drill operators:

1. Texas
2. Pennsylvania
3. Oklahoma
4. Wyoming
5. Louisiana

Top paying states for this profession:

1. Montana
2. New Jersey
3. Alaska
4. North Dakota
5. California

Wellhead pumper:

A wellhead pumper is a person who operates power pumps and auxiliary equipment to produce flow of oil or gas from wells in oil field. A wellhead pumper can be expected to monitor control panels, operate engines and pumps, perform routine maintenance, repair meters and gauges, and drive trucks to transport high pressure pumping equipment. Some of the skills required for this position are critical thinking, complex problem solving, operation monitoring, repairing, and decision making.

While some employers may expect a high school diploma to qualify an applicant, there are others who will hire applicants without one. 13% of wellhead pumpers do not have a high school diploma.

National Estimates:

Minimum annual salary:	$26,930
Average annual salary:	$46,140
Maximum annual salary:	$67,360

The 2 industries that have the highest levels of employment in this profession are oil and gas extraction and support activities for mining. Oil and gas extractors pay wellhead pumpers an average hourly wage of $22.69 an hour. Mining support companies pay wellhead pumpers an average hourly wage of $21.30 an hour.

The following are the top paying industries for this profession:

Industry Hourly mean wage

Industry	Hourly mean wage
Management of Companies and Enterprises	$26.18
Oil and Gas Extraction	$22.69
Support Activities for Mining	$21.30
Pipeline Transportation of Natural Gas	$21.23

States with the most employed wellhead pumpers:

1. Texas
2. Oklahoma
3. New Mexico
4. Pennsylvania
5. West Virginia

Top paying states for this profession:

1. California
2. North Dakota
3. Utah
4. Colorado
5. Louisiana

Service unit operator:

A service unit operator prepares the well and assembles the equipment that removes the oil or gas from the well. This person typically maintains the wells, observe load variations, inspect engines and rotary chains, operate pumps and controls, and drive truck-mounted unit to well sites. It is necessary that operators possess depth perception, good eye to hand coordination, interpersonal skills, physical strength, and being detail oriented in order to be effective at this position.

The typical level of education required for entry into oil and gas occupations is less than a high school diploma. However, some employers prefer to hire graduates of high school vocational programs in which students learn such skills as basic mechanics, welding, and heavy equipment operations. Most workers start as helpers to experienced workers and learn skills on the job.

National Estimates:

Minimum annual salary:	$28,190
Average annual salary:	$47,540
Maximum annual salary:	$72,890

The 2 industries that have the highest levels of employment in this profession are support activities for mining and oil and gas extraction. Mining support companies pay their operators an average hourly wage of $22.88 an hour. Oil and gas extractors pay their operators an average hourly wage of $23.00 an hour.

The following are the top paying industries for this profession:

Industry Hourly mean wage

Commercial and Industrial Machinery and Equipment Rental and Leasing	$31.62
Natural Gas Distribution	$24.26
Oil and Gas Extraction	$23.00
Support Activities for Mining	$22.88
Other Chemical Product and Preparation	$22.55

Manufacturing

States with the most employed service unit operators:

1. Texas
2. Louisiana
3. Oklahoma
4. Colorado
5. North Dakota

Top paying states for this profession:
- Florida
- North Dakota
- Alaska
- California
- New Mexico

Bridge and lock tenders:

A bridge and lock tender who operates and tend bridges, canal locks, and lighthouses to permit marine passage on inland waterways, near shores, and at danger points in waterway passages. This person may supervise such operations. A bridge and lock tender may be expected to move levers, control machinery, prepare accident reports, inspect canal and bridge equipment, and record information.

While some employers may expect a high school diploma to qualify an applicant, there are others who will hire applicants without one. 50% of bridge and lock tenders do not have a high school diploma.

National Estimates:

Minimum annual salary:	$24,530
Average annual salary:	$45,940
Maximum annual salary:	$57,320

The industry that has the highest levels of employment in this profession is rail transportation. Rail transportation companies pay their bridge and lock tenders an average hourly rate of $23.91 an hour.

The following are the top paying industries for this profession:

Industry Hourly mean wage

Federal Executive Branch	$24.66
Rail Transportation	$23.91

Support Activities for Water Transportation	$20.06
State Government	$17.87
Local Government	$17.39

States with the most employed bridge and lock tenders:

1. Louisiana
2. Michigan
3. Florida
4. New Jersey
5. Illinois

Top paying states for this profession:

1. Pennsylvania
2. Minnesota
3. Illinois
4. Missouri
5. Iowa

Tapers:

A taper prepares the wallboards for painting, using tape and other materials.

Tapers learn their trade informally by helping more experienced workers and gradually being given more duties. Employers usually give some on-the-job training that may last from 1 to 12 months. A few tapers may learn through a 3 or 4 year apprenticeship. During training, apprentices learn constructions basics related to blueprint reading, mathematics, building code requirements, safety, and first aid practices. After completing an apprenticeship program, tapers are considered journey workers and may perform duties on their own.

Although there are no formal education requirements to become a taper, high school math and general shop courses are considered useful.

National Estimates:

Minimum annual salary:	$20,240
Average annual salary:	$32,000
Maximum annual salary:	$45,470

The industry that has the highest levels of employment in this profession is electrical equipment manufacturing. Electric equipment manufacturers pay their tapers an average hourly wage of $15.97 an hour.

The following are the top paying industries for this profession:

Industry Hourly mean wage

Foundries	$24.73
Power Transmission Manufacturing	$20.96
Construction, Agriculture, and Mining Machinery Manufacturing	$18.67
Metalworking Machinery Manufacturing	$18.64
HVAC Equipment Manufacturing	$18.25

States with the most employed tapers:
1. California
2. Mississippi
3. Ohio
4. Texas
5. Pennsylvania

Top paying states for this profession:
1. Alabama
2. Georgia
3. Wisconsin
4. New Jersey
5. Colorado

Mine shuttle car operator:

A mine shuttle car operator is a person who operates diesel or electric-powered shuttle cars in underground mines to transport materials from the working face to mine cars or conveyors. Some of the tasks that these operators do are control machines, monitor processes, directing other workers, evaluating information, inspecting and repairing equipment.

There are no formal education requirements to become a mine shuttle car operator. Work experience in a related field is not required.

National Estimates:

Minimum annual salary:	$41,620
Average annual salary:	$51,310
Maximum annual salary:	$59,890

The industry that has the highest levels of employment in this profession is coal mining. Coal mining companies pay their operators an average hourly wage of $24.65 an hour.

The following are the top paying industries for this profession:

Industry Hourly mean wage

Nonmetallic Mineral Mining and Quarrying	$28.24
Coal Mining	$24.65

States with the most employed mine shuttle car operators:
1. West Virginia
2. Kentucky
3. Virginia
4. Pennsylvania
5. Illinois

Top paying states for this profession:
1. Wyoming
2. West Virginia
3. Pennsylvania
4. Alabama
5. Virginia

Tank car/truck/ship loaders:

A tank car/truck/ship loader is a person who load and unload chemicals and bulk solids, such as coal, sand, and grain into or from tank cars, trucks, or ships using material moving equipment. They may perform a variety of other tasks relating to shipment of products. They also may gauge or sample shipping tanks and test them for leaks.

Some employers prefer applicants with a high school diploma, but most simply require workers to be at least 18 years old and physically able to perform the work.

National Estimates:

Minimum annual salary:	$23,900
Average annual salary:	$46,400
Maximum annual salary:	$72,360

The 2 industries that have the highest levels of employment in this profession are support activities for water transportation and support activities for rail transportation. Water transportation companies pay their loaders an average hourly wage of $26.40 an hour, while rail transportation companies pay their loaders an average hourly wage of $19.20 an hour.

The following are the top paying industries for this profession:

Industry Hourly mean wage

Support Activities for Water Transportation	$26.40
Coal Mining	$23.23
Other Chemical Product Manufacturing	$22.53
Petroleum and Coal Products Manufacturing	$22.22
Warehousing and Storage	$21.88

States with the most employed tank car/truck/ship loaders:

1. Texas
2. New Jersey
3. Louisiana
4. Pennsylvania
5. Illinois

Top paying states for this profession:

1. Washington
2. New Jersey
3. Oregon
4. Wyoming
5. Alabama

Automotive technician:

An automotive tech is a person who inspects, maintains, and repairs cars and light trucks. These technicians work on traditional mechanical components, such as engines, transmissions, belts, and hoses. However, they must also be familiar with a growing number of electronic systems.

Braking, transmission, and steering systems, for example, are controlled primarily by computers and electronic components. Other integrated electronic systems, such as accident-avoidance sensors, are becoming common as well. In addition, a growing number of technicians are required to work on vehicles that run on alternative fuels, such as ethanol and electricity.

High school courses in automotive repair, electronics, computers, mathematics, and English provide a good background for prospective technicians. New workers generally start as trainee technicians, technicians' helpers, or lubrication workers and gradually acquire and practice their skills by working with experienced mechanics and technicians.

National Estimates:

Minimum annual salary:	$20,810
Average annual salary:	$39,060
Maximum annual salary:	$60,070

The 3 industries that have the highest levels of employment in this profession are automobile dealers, automobile repair and maintenance, and auto parts, accessories, and tire shops. Automobile dealers pay their technicians an average hourly wage of $20.79 an hour. Automobile repair and maintenance shops pay their technicians an average hourly wage of $17.00 an hour. Auto parts and tire shops pay their technicians an average hourly wage of $16.27 an hour.

The following are the top paying industries for this profession:

Industry Hourly mean wage

Aerospace Product and Parts Manufacturing	$33.43
Natural Gas Distribution	$30.27
Scientific Research and Development Services	$28.83
Couriers and Express Delivery Services	$28.28
Wired Telecommunications Carriers	$27.71

States with the most employed automotive technicians:

1. California
2. Texas
3. Florida

4. New York
5. Pennsylvania

Top paying states for this profession:
1. Alaska
2. District of Columbia
3. Hawaii
4. New Jersey
5. California

Welder:

A welder is a person who uses hand-welding to weld metal components. Welders work in a wide variety of industries, from car racing to manufacturing. The work that welders do and the equipment they use vary, depending on the industry. The most common and simplest type of welding today, arc welding, uses electrical currents to create heat and bond metals together—but there are more than 100 different processes that a welder can use.

Formal training is available in high school technical education courses. Some employers are willing to hire inexperienced entry-level workers and train them on the job.

National Estimates:

Minimum annual salary:	$24,720
Average annual salary:	$38,410
Maximum annual salary:	$56,130

The 2 industries that have the highest levels of employment in this profession are motor vehicle body and trailer manufacturing and architectural and structural metals manufacturing. Motor vehicle body and trailer manufacturers pay their welders an average hourly wage of

$16.07 an hour. Architectural and structural metals manufacturers pay their welders an average hourly wage of $16.98 an hour.

The following are the top paying industries for this profession:

Industry	Hourly mean wage
Electric Power Generation, Distribution, and Transmission	$30.21
Scheduled Air Transportation	$28.50
Natural Gas Distribution	$28.37
Pulp, Paper, and Paperboard Mills	$28.30
Metal Ore Mining	$27.47

States with the most employed welders:
1. Texas
2. California
3. Pennsylvania
4. Louisiana
5. Ohio

Top paying states for this profession:
1. Alaska
2. Hawaii
3. District of Columbia
4. Wyoming
5. Maryland

Carpenter:

A carpenter is a person who constructs and repairs building frameworks and structures, such as stairways, doorframes, partitions, and rafters, made from wood and other materials. They also may install kitchen cabinets, siding, and drywall.

Carpenters use many different hand and power tools to cut and shape wood, plastic, fiberglass, or drywall. They commonly use hand tools, including squares, levels, and chisels, as well as many power tools, such as sanders, circular saws, and nail guns. Carpenters put materials together with nails, screws, staples, and adhesives, and do a final check of their work to ensure accuracy. They use a tape measure on every project because proper measuring increases productivity, reduces waste, and ensures that the pieces being cut are the proper size.

Although most carpenters learn their trade through a formal apprenticeship, some learn on the job, starting as a helper.

National Estimates:

Minimum annual salary:	$24,880
Average annual salary:	$44,520
Maximum annual salary:	$72,580

The 3 industries that have the highest levels of employment in this profession are residential building construction, nonresidential building construction, and building finishing contractors. Nonresidential building construction contractors pay their carpenters an average hourly wage of $23.04 an hour. Building finishing contractors pay their carpenters an average hourly wage of $22.02 an hour. Residential building construction companies pay their carpenters an average hourly wage of $20.15 an hour.

The following are the top paying industries for this profession:

Industry Hourly mean wage

Motion Picture and Video Industries	$33.22
Investigation and Security Services	$29.78
Promoters of Performing Arts and Sports	$29.17

Specialty Hospitals	$28.46
Performing Arts Companies	$27.75

States with the most employed carpenters:
1. California
2. New York
3. Pennsylvania
4. Texas
5. Florida

Top paying states for this profession:
1. Hawaii
2. Alaska
3. New York
4. Massachusetts
5. California

Diesel mechanic:

A diesel mechanic is a person that inspects, repairs, or overhauls buses, trucks, and anything else with a diesel engine. Diesel mechanics handle many kinds of repairs. They may work on a vehicle's electrical system, make major engine repairs, or retrofit engines with emission control systems to comply with pollution regulations.

Some diesel mechanics begin working without postsecondary education and are trained on the job. Trainees are assigned basic tasks, such as cleaning parts, checking fuel and oil levels, and driving vehicles in and out of the shop. After they learn routine maintenance and repair tasks and demonstrate competence, trainees move on to more complicated jobs. This process can last from 3 to 4 years, at which point a trainee is usually considered a journey-level diesel mechanic.

National Estimates:

Minimum annual salary:	$26,820
Average annual salary:	$43,660
Maximum annual salary:	$63,520

The 3 industries that have the highest levels of employment in this profession are motor vehicle parts and supplier wholesalers, general freight trucking, and specialized freight trucking.

Parts and supplier wholesalers pay their diesel mechanics an average hourly wage of $21.06 an hour. General and specialized freight trucking companies pay their diesel mechanics an average hourly wage of $19.20 (G) and $18.50 (S) an hour.

The following are the top paying industries for this profession:

Industry Hourly mean wage

Water Transportation	$38.10
Federal Executive Branch	$33.08
Couriers and Express Delivery Services	$28.72
Electric Power Generation, Transmission, and Distribution	$28.58
Scientific Research and Development Services	$28.52

States with the most employed diesel mechanics:

1. Texas
2. California
3. New York
4. Ohio
5. Pennsylvania

Top paying states for this profession:
1. Hawaii
2. Alaska
3. Wyoming
4. Nevada
5. Connecticut

CDL Truck Driver:

A CDL truck driver is a person who transports goods from one location to another. Most drivers are long-haul drivers and operate trucks with a capacity of at least 26,001 pounds per gross vehicle weight (GVW). They deliver goods over intercity routes, sometimes spanning several states. Some heavy truck drivers transport hazardous materials, such as chemical waste, and so have to take special precautions when driving.

Some companies may require their truck drivers to have a high school diploma or equivalent but a commercial driver's license is the main requirement. Some drivers attend professional driving schools, where they take training courses to learn how to maneuver large vehicles on highways or through crowded streets. During these classes, drivers also learn the federal laws and regulations governing interstate truck driving.

Drivers can get endorsements to their CDL that show their ability to drive a specialized type of vehicle. Truck drivers transporting hazardous materials (HAZMAT) must have a hazardous materials endorsement (H). Getting this endorsement requires an additional knowledge test and a background check.

National Estimates:

Minimum annual salary:	$25,110
Average annual salary:	$40,360
Maximum annual salary:	$58,910

The 3 industries that have the highest levels of employment in this profession are general freight trucking, specialized freight trucking, and cement and concrete product manufacturing. General and specialized freight trucking companies pay their drivers an average hourly wage of $20.04 (G) and $19.19 (S) an hour. Cement and concrete product manufacturers pay their drivers an average hourly wage of $17.82 an hour.

The following are the top paying industries for this profession:

Industry Hourly mean wage

Other Electrical Equipment Manufacturing	$31.24
Transportation Equipment Manufacturing	$29.95
Courier and Express Delivery Services	$27.95
Aerospace Product and Parts Manufacturing	$27.29
Postal Service	$25.37

States with the most employed CDL truck drivers:
1. Texas
2. California
3. Pennsylvania
4. Florida
5. Ohio

Top paying states for this profession:
1. Alaska
2. Massachusetts
3. North Dakota
4. Nevada
5. Wyoming

Painter:

A painter is a person who applies paint, stain, and coatings to walls, buildings, bridges, and other structures.

There is no formal educational requirement, but high school courses in English, math, shop, and blueprint reading can be useful. Although most painters learn their trade informally on the job, some learn through a formal apprenticeship. While the vast majority of workers learn their trade informally on the job or through a formal apprenticeship, some contractors offer their own training program.

National Estimates:

Minimum annual salary:	$22,980
Average annual salary:	$38,590
Maximum annual salary:	$60,240

The 2 industries that have the highest levels of employment in this profession are building finishing contractors and residential building construction. Building finishing contractors pay their painters an average hourly wage of $18.01 an hour. Residential building construction companies pay their painters an average hourly wage of $17.44 an hour.

The following are the top paying industries for this profession:

Industry Hourly mean wage

Motion Picture and Video Industries	$32.24
Electric Power Generation, Transmission, and Distribution	$29.86
Accounting, Tax Prep, and Payroll Services	$26.87
Postal Service	$26.49
Specialty Hospitals	$25.20

States with the most employed painters:
1. California
2. Texas
3. Florida
4. New York
5. Illinois

Top paying states for this profession:
1. Illinois
2. Hawaii
3. Alaska
4. District of Columbia
5. New York

It is true that all of these professions are blue collar careers. These professions require a person to be in good physical condition and possess a great work ethic. While the work may be not considered fun or exciting, it offers a desirable salary for a high school dropout.

Then, you have another group of people who don't want to get their hands dirty and would rather have a corporate job. I'm not implying that it's impossible to get one without a high school diploma. What I can assure you is that it won't be an easy task. After all, you can't expect to have the world when you have nothing to offer.

Quasi-millionaires with no high school diploma
1. Mike Hudack (founder of Blip.tv, now Facebook product manager)

Multimillionaires with no high school diploma
1. Robert Dinero (actor)
2. David Karp (Founder of Tumblr)

3. Quentin Tarantino (film director, producer, and actor)
4. Jessica Simpson (singer and actress)
5. Uma Thurman (actress)
6. Larry Flynt (publisher)
7. Billy Joel (singer)
8. Tom Cruise (actor)
9. Don Imus (syndicated radio show host)
10. Jay-Z (rapper)
11. George Foreman (boxer)
12. David Murdock (chairman and CEO of Dole Foods)
13. Jim Clark (founder of Netscape)
14. Avril Lavigne (singer)
15. Cameron Diaz (actress)
16. Charlie Sheen (actor)
17. Catherine Zeta Jones (actress)
18. Elton John (singer)
19. Christina Applegate (actress)
20. Jim Carrey (actor)
21. Drew Barrymore (actress)
22. John Travolta (actor)
23. Johnny Depp (actor)
24. Hilary Swank (actress)
25. Mark Wahlberg (actor)
26. Nicholas Cage (actor)
27. Lindsey Lohan (singer and actress)
28. Ryan Gosling (actor)
29. Eminem (rapper and actor)
30. Seth Rogan (actor)
31. Al Pacino (actor)
32. Whoopi Goldberg (actress and TV show host)
33. Peter Jennings (news anchor and author)

<u>Billionaires with no high school diploma</u>
1. Richard Branson (CEO of Virgin)
2. Kirk Kerkorian (CEO of Tracinda)
3. Carl Henry Linder Jr. (Former CEO of Cincinnati Reds)

CHAPTER 4

Land a Career without a College Degree

So, you have a high school diploma. You are not alone. Most Americans do (200+ million actually). Forty years ago, having a high school diploma was enough to get a decent job. Nowadays, a high school diploma will barely yield you a great career unless you read Chapter 3 (wink, wink). Twenty years ago, our parents' advice was to go to college because once we have that degree is when we also get the great career.

Here we are now in the 21st century with more students than ever enrolling in college. How valuable is a college degree nowadays?

Srikant Vasan, founder and president of Portmont College at Mount St. Mary's, says "the return on investment in college education clearly goes down as the return decreases with the decreasing probability of finding employment, especially employment at higher salaries, and investment increases with the rising costs of college.... students should check out alternatives to college degrees."

How valuable is a college degree if one-third of the courses are irrelevant to the major?

Two new studies from the Community College Research Center at Columbia University's Teachers College have found that community colleges unnecessarily place tens of thousands of entering students in remedial classes. At most community colleges, a majority of entering students who recently graduated from high school are placed in remedial classes, where they pay tuition but earn no college credit.

Occidental College offers a course called Stupidity. The course examines the stupidity felt in political life, ranging from the presidency to Beavis and Butthead. How does the course help a political science major or any other college student?

New York University offers a course called The Thingliness of Things. The course engages a seemingly simple question: What is a thing? How is the course appropriate for any college student?

Ohio State University offers a course called Sport for the Spectator. The course is defined as the study of various popular spectator sports. How does the course help a sports management major or any other college student?

Reed College offers a course called The Death of Satan. The course teaches students why Americans no longer fear Satan and how they lost their sense of evil. This course would probably suitable for religion majors. So, why is it in the English major curriculum?

Stanford University offers a course called Technology and Culture: Virtual People. The course teaches students about the importance of having a really good looking avatar in social networking situations and virtual worlds. You can continue reading after you're finished laughing.

The University of Virginia offers a course called GaGa for Gaga: Sex, Gender, and Identity. The course analyzes how the musician pushes social boundaries with her work. From the description, it sounds like an interesting class but it's still not relevant to any major.

The University of South Carolina offers a course called Lady Gaga and The Sociology of Fame. The course unravels the sociologically relevant dimensions of the fame of Lady Gaga with respect to her music, videos, fashion, and other artistic endeavors. Another interesting class… I'm just wondering how many employers are going to be impressed about these graduates' knowledge of Lady Gaga.

The University of Texas offers a course called Invented Languages: Klingon and Beyond. A course on this topic is absolutely unnecessary. Anyone who wants to learn Klingon should just watch Star Trek.

Columbia College offers a course called Zombies in Popular Media. This course explores the history, significance, and representation of the zombie as a figure of a horror and fantasy texts. So, do we expect students to apply this fiction in the real world?

Swarthmore College requires film and media students to take a course called Conspiracy. The course teaches students about paranoia and conspiracy theories in film and television. How does the course help a film and media student?

Bennington College requires anthropology students to take a course called Reading The Body. The course teaches students why most people want to look some ways and other people want to look other ways. How is the course appropriate for any college student?

The University of New York at Buffalo offers a course called Cyberporn and Society. As unusual as it sounds, the bulk of the course requires students to survey porn sites. This seems to be more of a college student's fantasy than a required course in a college curriculum.

Andy Kessler, who was interviewed about the topic on CNBC, stated that his son was required to take foreign language courses, despite the fact that he was a computer science major. He quoted his son saying to the university's registrar, "The internet is English and Google Translate can do everything else." Despite the truth of the matter, he was still required to take a set of foreign language courses.

In 2010, recent college graduates left school owing an average of $25,250 in student loans--the highest amount ever. According to the Federal Reserve Board of New York, 37 million Americans currently have outstanding student loans. The frustration with the economy and high unemployment rates is consistently shaping public opinion about college degrees, which traditionally was thought of as safeguards against unemployment. Now, a degree can no longer guarantee a college graduate a lucrative career.

While college graduates do stand a better chance of landing a job than those who don't graduate, they are being left with jobs that would also be offered to a person without a degree. 1 in 3 college graduates has a job historically performed by those with a high school diploma or a GED. Over 284,000 college graduates had minimum wage jobs last year. As students graduate with a huge debt burden, it is these types of jobs that will make living difficult for them. The Associated Press found that half of young college graduates are either jobless or underemployed.

Some experts argue that attending college has become less about learning actual skills and more about simply paying to have a degree. According to Time Magazine, 36% of students failed to demonstrate any improved learning in their 4 year study.

Simply put, college is not for everybody. William Bennett, author of Is College Worth It, says "they should stop and think. It's not like deciding to have breakfast or going to bed. It's more like getting married. It's a big decision." If a person plans on working in a career that is related to their major, it is important that they study a major that has high demand in the workforce. Only 27% of college graduates have a job related to their major. The data also shows that your chances of finding a job related to your degree goes up when you move to a big city.

So, why should a student go to college for a degree to work a job that is not relevant to their studies? That's not the reason why students go to college. Living in an era with a struggling economy has forced students to reconsider their options. Is it worth paying thousands of dollars for a degree that is not relevant to your career? Some people have already seen this trend and decided to skip college. Others have caught on and decided to drop out of college.

So, let's take a look at the professions that don't require a college degree. Most of these professions require you to be in good physical condition to be considered for the position.

Plumbers:

A plumber is a person who installs and repairs water, drainage, and gas pipes in homes, businesses, and factories. Plumbers also install plumbing fixtures—bathtubs, showers, sinks, and toilets—and appliances such as dishwashers, garbage disposals, and water heaters as well as addressing plumbing problems.

Most plumbers learn on the job through an apprenticeship. A 4 or 5 year apprenticeship is how most plumbers learn their trade. Each year, apprentices must have at least 1,700 to 2,000 hours of paid on-the-job training and a minimum of 246 hours of related technical education. Some start out by attending a technical school. After completing an apprenticeship program, plumbers are considered to be a journey worker, which qualifies them to perform duties on their own.

Most states and localities require plumbers to have a license. Although licensing requirements vary, most states and localities require workers to have 2 to 5 years of experience and to pass an exam that tests their knowledge of the trade and of local plumbing codes before they are permitted to work independently. Check with your state licensing board.

National Estimates

Minimum annual salary:	$29,020
Average annual salary:	$52,950
Maximum annual salary:	$84,440

The 3 industries that have the highest levels of employment in this profession are building equipment contractors, ship and boat building, and utility system construction.

Ship and boat building companies pay their plumbers an average hourly wage of $22.65 an hour. Utility system construction companies pay their plumbers an average hourly wage of $23.50 an hour. Building equipment contractors pay their plumbers an average hourly wage of $25.76 an hour.

The following are the top paying industries for this profession:

Industry Hourly mean wage

Electric Power Generation, Transmission, and Distribution	$32.84

States with the most employed plumbers:
1. Texas
2. California
3. New York
4. Pennsylvania
5. Florida

Top paying states for this profession:
1. Alaska
2. New York
3. Illinois
4. Massachusetts
5. New Jersey

Locksmiths:

A locksmith is a person who repair and open locks, make keys, change locks and safe combinations, and install and repair safes.

The typical entry-level education is a high school diploma or GED. 61% of locksmiths have no college degree. Work experience in this field or a related field is helpful but not at all required. These positions usually provide long term on-the-job training.

National Estimates

Minimum annual salary:	$22,060
Average annual salary:	$39,160
Maximum annual salary:	$59,110

The 1 industry that has the highest levels of employment in this profession is investigation and security services. Investigate and security companies pay their locksmiths an average hourly wage of $17.65 an hour.

The following are the top paying industries for this profession:

Industry Hourly mean wage

Junior Colleges	$24.53

States with the most employed locksmiths:
1. California
2. Florida
3. Texas
4. New York
5. Ohio

Top paying states for this profession:
1. District of Columbia
2. Hawaii

3. Massachusetts
4. New Jersey
5. Nevada

Tile and Marble Setters:

Tile and marble setters are people who apply tiles or marble to walls, floors, and other surfaces. They install materials on a variety of surfaces, such as floors, walls, ceilings, countertops, patios, and roof decks.

Several groups, including unions and contractor associations, sponsor apprenticeship programs. The basic qualifications for entering an apprenticeship program are to be eighteen years of age, a high school diploma or equivalent, and physically able to perform the work. Although some tile and marble setters learn their trade through a formal apprenticeship, many learn informally on the job, starting as a helper.

National Estimates

Minimum annual salary:	$21,450
Average annual salary:	$41,820
Maximum annual salary:	$70,970

The 2 industries that have the highest levels of employment in this profession are building finishing contractors and other nonmetallic mineral product manufacturers. Building finishing contractors pay their tile and marble setters an average hourly wage of $20.03 an hour. Nonmetallic mineral product manufacturers pay their tile and marble setters an average hourly wage of $17.38 an hour.

The following are the top paying industries for this profession:

Industry Hourly mean wage	
Foundation, Structure, and Building Exterior Contractors	$25.32

States with the most employed tile and marble setters:
1. California
2. Florida
3. Texas
4. New York
5. Arizona

Top paying states for this profession:
1. Massachusetts
2. New York
3. Hawaii
4. Connecticut
5. New Jersey

Pest control workers:

A pest control worker is a person who control, manage, or remove unwanted creatures, such as roaches, rats, ants, termites, and bedbugs, that infest buildings and surrounding areas.

State laws require pest control workers to be licensed. Most workers need a high school diploma and receive on-the-job training, which usually lasts less than 3 months. Many pest control companies require that employees have good driving records. Most pest control workers begin as technicians, receiving both formal technical instruction and on-the-job training from employers. Pest control workers typically advance as they gain experience. Some experienced workers start their own pest management company.

National Estimates

Minimum annual salary:	$19,540
Average annual salary:	$32,190
Maximum annual salary:	$47,770

The 1 industry that has the highest levels of employment in this profession is building and dwelling services. Building service companies pay their pest control workers an average hourly wage of $15.33 an hour.

The following are the top paying industries for this profession:

Industry Hourly mean wage

Facilities Support Services	$19.72

States with the most employed pest control workers:
1. California
2. Florida
3. Texas
4. Georgia
5. New York

Top paying states for this profession:
1. Massachusetts
2. District of Columbia
3. Wyoming
4. Washington
5. Montana

Vending and Amusement Machine Servicers:

A vending or amusement machine servicer is a person who install, service, adjust, or repair coin, vending, or amusement machines, including video games, jukeboxes, pinball machines, or slot machines.

The typical entry-level education is a high school diploma or GED. 87% of vending and amusement machine servicers have no college degree. Work experience in this field or a related field is helpful but not at all required. These positions usually provide short term on-the-job training.

National Estimates

Minimum annual salary:	$19,150
Average annual salary:	$32,700
Maximum annual salary:	$47,760

The 2 industries that have the highest levels of employment in this profession are vending machine operators and beverage manufacturers. Vending machine companies pay their servicers an average hourly wage of $14.30 an hour. Beverage manufacturers pay their servicers an average hourly wage of $16.56 an hour.

The following are the top paying industries for this profession:

Industry Hourly mean wage

Traveler Accommodation	$20.44
Other Miscellaneous Manufacturing	$19.47
Commercial and Service Machinery	$19.39

States with the most employed vending and amusement machine servicer:

1. California
2. Texas
3. New York
4. Pennsylvania
5. Ohio

Top paying states for this profession:
1. New Jersey
2. Nevada
3. Oregon
4. Massachusetts
5. Idaho

Forest and Conservation Workers:

A forest or conservation worker is a person who measure and improve the quality of forests. Under the supervision of foresters and forest and conservation technicians, they help to develop, maintain, and protect forests. Forest and conservation workers typically plant seedlings to reforest land, clear away debris from trails, count trees, identify and removing diseased trees, spraying trees with insecticides and fungicides, and inject vegetation with insecticides and herbicides.

Forest and conservation workers typically need a high school diploma before they begin working. Entry-level forest and conservation workers generally get on-the-job training as they help more experienced workers. They do routine labor-intensive tasks, such as planting or thinning trees. When the opportunity arises, they learn from experienced technicians and foresters who do more complex tasks, such as gathering data.

National Estimates

Minimum annual salary:	$16,690
Average annual salary:	$28,600
Maximum annual salary:	$45,900

The 3 industries that have the highest levels of employment in this profession are state government, social advocacy and logging organizations.

State government pay forest and conservation workers an average hourly wage of $12.46 an hour. Social advocacy organizations pay their forest and conservation workers an average hourly wage of $12.54 an hour. Logging companies pay their forest and conservation workers an average hourly wage of $16.42 an hour.

The following are the top paying industries for this profession:

Industry Hourly mean wage

Logging	$16.42
Sawmills and Wood Preservation	$14.03

States with the most employed forest and conservation workers:
1. California
2. Georgia
3. South Dakota
4. Washington
5. Louisiana

Top paying states for this profession:
1. Pennsylvania
2. Wisconsin
3. Missouri
4. Massachusetts
5. Alabama

Logging Workers:

A logging worker is a person who harvests acres of forest. The timber they harvest provides the raw material for countless consumer and industrial products. Logging workers typically cut down trees, fasten chains around logs, separate logs by species, drive tractors, and grade logs according to their characteristics.

Most logging workers have a high school diploma. They get on-the-job training to become familiar with forest environments and to learn how to operate logging machinery. Many states have training programs for loggers. Although specific coursework may vary by state, most programs usually include technical instruction or field training in a number of areas, including best management practices, environmental compliance, and reforestation.

National Estimates

Minimum annual salary:	$20,780
Average annual salary:	$34,650
Maximum annual salary:	$46,580

The 2 industries that have the highest levels of employment in this profession are logging and sawmills and wood preservation. Logging companies pay their workers an average hourly wage of $16.83 an hour. Sawmills and wood preservation companies pay their workers an average hourly wage of $15.07 an hour.

The following are the top paying industries for this profession:

Industry Hourly mean wage

Logging	$16.83
Sawmills and Wood Preservation	$15.07

States with the most employed logging workers:

1. Oregon
2. Washington
3. Georgia
4. California
5. New York

Top paying states for this profession:
1. Maine
2. Alabama
3. Michigan
4. Oregon
5. Texas

Fashion designers:

A fashion designer is a person who creates original clothing, accessories, and footwear. They sketch designs, select fabrics and patterns, and give instructions on how to make the products they designed. Some fashion designers specialize in clothing, footwear, or accessory design, but others create designs in all three fashion categories.

Postsecondary education is not required. Employers usually seek applicants with creativity, as well as a good technical understanding of the production process for clothing, accessories, or footwear. Fashion designers often gain their initial experience in the fashion industry through internships or by working as an assistant designer. Internships provide aspiring fashion designers an opportunity to experience the design process, building their knowledge of textiles, colors, and how the industry works.

Beginning fashion designers usually start out as patternmakers or sketching assistants to more experienced designers before advancing to higher level positions.

National Estimates

Minimum annual salary:	$34,110
Average annual salary:	$72,620
Maximum annual salary:	$126,290

The 3 industries that have the highest levels of employment in this profession are apparel merchant wholesalers, cut and sew apparel manufacturers, and specialized design servicers.

Cut and sew apparel manufacturers pay their fashion designers an average hourly wage of $35.16 an hour. Specialized design servicers pay their fashion designers an average hourly wage of $35.11 an hour. Apparel merchant wholesalers pay their fashion designers an average hourly wage of $33.91 an hour.

The following are the top paying industries for this profession:

Industry Hourly mean wage

Footwear Manufacturing	$35.67
Cut and Sew Apparel Manufacturing	$35.16
Specialized Design Services	$35.11

States with the most employed fashion designers:
1. New York
2. California
3. Texas
4. Ohio
5. New Jersey

Top paying states for this profession:
1. Maine
2. New York
3. Ohio
4. Missouri
5. California

Telecommunications installers / repairers:

Telecommunications installers and repairers, also known as telecom techs, set up and maintain devices or equipment that carry communications signals, connect to telephone lines, or access the Internet.

Telecom techs can get training through a certificate program in electronics repair, computer science, or related areas. Because technology in this field evolves quickly, telecom techs must continue to educate themselves over the course of their careers. They may attend manufacturers' training classes, read equipment manuals, or get hands-on experience with the latest equipment.

National Estimates

Minimum annual salary:	$30,840
Average annual salary:	$53,710
Maximum annual salary:	$75,040

The 3 industries that have the highest levels of employment in this profession are wired telecommunications carriers, cable and subscription programmers, and other telecommunications.

Cable and subscription programmers pay their telecom techs an average hourly wage of $24.87 an hour. Wired telecommunications carriers pay their telecom techs an average hourly wage of $26.30 an hour. Other telecommunications companies pay their telecom techs an average hourly wage of $30.03 an hour.

The following are the top paying industries for this profession:

Industry Hourly mean wage

Natural Gas Distribution	$36.72
Computer Systems Design and Related Services	$30.88

States with the most employed telecom techs:
1. California
2. Texas
3. Florida
4. New York
5. Georgia

Top paying states for this profession:
1. Rhode Island
2. New Jersey
3. New York
4. Alaska
5. District of Columbia

Glaziers:

A glazier is a person who installs glass in windows, skylights, storefronts, and display cases to create distinctive designs or reduce the need for artificial lighting. Glaziers typically follow blueprints or specifications to be used, remove any old or broken glass, cut glass to the specified size and shape, make or install sashes or moldings for glass installation.

Glaziers typically enter the occupation with a high school diploma or GED, and learn their trade through a formal apprenticeship. The typical training for glaziers is a 3-year apprenticeship. Each year, apprentices must have at least 144 hours of related technical training and 2,000 hours of paid on-the-job training. After completing their apprenticeship, glaziers are considered to be journey workers who may do tasks on their own. Connecticut is the only state that requires licensure for glaziers.

National Estimates

Minimum annual salary:	$24,170
Average annual salary:	$42,090
Maximum annual salary:	$69,120

The 2 industries that have the highest levels of employment in this profession are foundation, structure, and building exterior contractors and glass and glass product manufacturers.

Foundation, structure, and building exterior contractors pay their glaziers an average hourly wage of $21.22 an hour. Glass and glass product manufacturers pay their glaziers an average hourly wage of $17.01 an hour.

The following are the top paying industries for this profession:

Industry Hourly mean wage

Residential Building Construction	$22.74

States with the most employed glaziers:
1. California
2. Texas
3. New York
4. Florida
5. Washington

Top paying states for this profession:
1. Missouri
2. Illinois
3. Connecticut
4. Oregon
5. New Jersey

Automobile Body Technicians:

An automobile body technician is a person who restores, refinish, and replaces vehicle bodies and frames, windshields, and window glass. Automotive body technicians can repair most damage from everyday vehicle collisions and make vehicles look and drive like new. Damage may be minor, such as replacing a cracked windshield, or major, such as replacing an entire door panel.

Many new auto body techs begin work without formal training. Although it is not required, postsecondary education can often be the best preparation. New workers typically begin their on-the-job training by helping an experienced auto body technician with basic tasks. As they gain experience, they move on to more complex work. Some workers may become trained in as little as a 1 year, but generally, workers may need 3 to 4 years of hands-on training to become fully qualified auto body technicians.

To keep up with rapidly changing automotive technology, auto body techs need to continue their education and training throughout their careers. They are expected to develop their skills by reading technical manuals and by attending classes and seminars. Many employers regularly send workers to advanced training programs. Although not required, certification is recommended because it shows competence and usually brings higher pay. In some instances, however, it is required for advancement beyond entry-level work.

National Estimates

Minimum annual salary:	$22,530
Average annual salary:	$41,840
Maximum annual salary:	$65,390

The 2 industries that have the highest levels of employment in this profession are automobile repair and maintenance shops and automobile dealers. Auto repair shops pay their techs an average hourly wage of

$19.78 an hour. Automobile dealers pay their techs an average hourly wage of $21.26 an hour.

The following are the top paying industries for this profession:

Industry Hourly mean wage

Motor Vehicle Manufacturing	$27.63
Spectator Sports	$27.34

States with the most employed auto body technicians:
1. California
2. Texas
3. Illinois
4. New York
5. Florida

Top paying states for this profession:
1. Alaska
2. District of Columbia
3. Maryland
4. Minnesota
5. Michigan

Executive administrative assistants:

An executive administrative assistant is a person who provides high-level administrative support for an office and for top executives of an organization. They often handle more complex responsibilities, such as reviewing incoming documents, conducting research, preparing reports, and arranging meetings. They may supervise clerical staff.

High school graduates who have office and computer skills usually qualify for entry-level positions. Employers of more specialized positions, often require applicants to have some knowledge of industry-specific terminology and practices. Although it is not required, certification can demonstrate competency to employers.

Administrative assistants generally advance through promotion to other administrative positions with more responsibilities. Qualified administrative assistants who broaden their knowledge of a company's operations and enhance their skills may be promoted to executive secretary or office manager.

National Estimates

Minimum annual salary:	$31,310
Average annual salary:	$50,220
Maximum annual salary:	$73,530

The 4 industries that have the highest levels of employment in this profession are local government, state government, management of companies and enterprises, and higher education institutions.

State government pays their assistants an average hourly wage of $21.05 an hour. Higher education institutions pay their assistants an average hourly wage of $22.82 an hour. Local government pays their assistants an average hourly wage of $24.50 an hour. Company and enterprise management firms pay their assistants an average hourly wage of $26.42 an hour.

The following are the top paying industries for this profession:

Industry Hourly mean wage

Securities and Commodities Exchanges	$31.40
Independent Artists, Writers, and Performers	$30.73
Other Financial Investment Activities	$30.27

States with the most employed executive administrative assistants:

1. California
2. Texas

3. New York
4. Florida
5. Illinois

Top paying states for this profession:
1. New York
2. New Jersey
3. Connecticut
4. Maryland
5. California

Bookkeepers:

A bookkeeper is a person who is often responsible for some or all of an organization's accounts, known as the general ledger. They record all transactions and post debits (costs) and credits (income). They also produce financial statements and other reports for supervisors and managers. Bookkeepers prepare bank deposits by compiling data from cashiers, verifying receipts, and sending cash, checks, or other forms of payment to the bank. In addition, they may handle payroll, make purchases, prepare invoices, and keep track of overdue accounts.

Most bookkeepers need a high school diploma, and they usually learn some of their skills on the job. They must have basic math and computer skills, including knowledge of spreadsheets and bookkeeping software. Some bookkeepers become certified.

The Certified Bookkeeper (CB) designation, awarded by the American Institute of Professional Bookkeepers, shows that people have the skills and knowledge needed to carry out all bookkeeping tasks, including overseeing payroll and balancing accounts, according to accepted accounting procedures. For certification, candidates must have at least 2 years of bookkeeping experience, pass a four-part exam, and adhere to a code of ethics.

The National Bookkeepers Association also offers certification. The Uniform Bookkeeper Certification Examination is an online test with 50 multiple-choice questions. Test takers must answer 80 percent of the questions correctly to pass the exam.

With appropriate experience and education, some bookkeepers may become accountants or auditors.

National Estimates

Minimum annual salary:	$21,610
Average annual salary:	$36,640
Maximum annual salary:	$54,310

The 4 industries that have the highest levels of employment in this profession are local government, depository credit intermediation, management of companies and enterprises, and accounting, tax preparation, bookkeeping, and payroll services.

Depository credit intermediation companies pay their bookkeepers an average hourly wage of $16.79 an hour. Accounting, tax preparation, bookkeeping, and payroll service companies pay their bookkeepers an average hourly wage of $17.37 an hour. Local government pays their bookkeepers an average hourly wage of $17.89 an hour. Company and enterprise management firms pay their bookkeepers an average hourly wage of $18.02 an hour.

The following are the top paying industries for this profession:

Industry Hourly mean wage

Motion Picture and Video Industries	$22.52
Securities and Commodity Contracts, Intermediation and Brokerage	$21.81

States with the most employed bookkeepers:
1. California
2. Texas
3. New York
4. Florida
5. Pennsylvania

Top paying states for this profession:
1. New York
2. Connecticut
3. Alaska
4. Massachusetts
5. California

Skincare specialists:

A skincare specialist is a person who cleanses and beautifies the face and body to enhance a person's appearance. They give facials, full-body treatments, and head and neck massages to improve the health and appearance of the skin. Some may provide other skincare treatments, such as peels, masks, or scrubs, to remove dead or dry skin.

In addition to working with clients, skincare specialists also keep records of skincare regimens that their regular clients use. A growing number of specialists actively sell skincare products, such as cleansers, lotions, and creams.

Skincare specialists usually take a state-approved cosmetology program. Some high schools offer vocational training. Most people receive their training from a postsecondary vocational school. Newly hired specialists sometimes receive on-the-job training, especially when working with chemicals. Those who are employed in a medical environment may also receive on-the-job training, often working alongside an experienced skincare specialist. After completing the program, they must pass a state exam for licensure, which all states require except Connecticut. Many states offer continuing education to keep skincare specialists current on new techniques and products.

National Estimates

Minimum annual salary:	$17,460
Average annual salary:	$31,720
Maximum annual salary:	$51,900

The 1 industry that has the highest levels of employment in this profession is personal care services. Personal care service companies pay their specialists an average hourly wage of $14.40 an hour.

The following are the top paying industries for this profession:

Industry Hourly mean wage

Offices of Physicians	$18.95

States with the most employed skincare specialists:
1. California
2. Texas
3. Florida
4. New York
5. Massachusetts

Top paying states for this profession:
1. Alaska
2. Oregon
3. District of Columbia
4. New Hampshire
5. Arkansas

Building inspectors:

A building inspector is a person who ensures that new construction, changes, or repairs comply with local and national building codes and ordinances, zoning regulations, and contract specifications. They also check the structural quality and general safety of buildings. Some specialize in structural steel or reinforced-concrete structures.

Most employers require building inspectors to have at least a high school diploma and considerable knowledge of construction trades. Building inspectors receive much of their training on the job, although they must learn building codes and standards on their own.

Many states and local jurisdictions require some type of license or certification. Some states have individual licensing programs for construction and building inspectors. Others may require certification by associations such as the International Code Council, International Association of Plumbing and Mechanical Officials, International Association of Electrical Inspectors, and National Fire Protection Association.

National Estimates

Minimum annual salary:	$32,050
Average annual salary:	$55,230
Maximum annual salary:	$83,760

The 1 industry that has the highest levels of employment in this profession is architectural, engineering, and related services. These types of companies pay their inspectors an average hourly wage of $25.99 an hour.

The following are the top paying industries for this profession:

Industry Hourly mean wage

Electric Power Generation, Transmission, and Distribution	$35.41
Natural Gas Distribution	$33.36
Federal Executive Branch	$31.82

States with the most employed building inspectors:
1. California
2. Texas
3. New York
4. Florida
5. Pennsylvania

Top paying states for this profession:
1. District of Columbia
2. California
3. Nevada
4. Alaska
5. Washington

Electricians:

An electrician is a person who installs and maintains electrical systems in homes, businesses, and factories. They read blueprints, which are technical diagrams of electrical systems that show the location of circuits, outlets, and other equipment. They use different types of hand and power tools, such as pipe benders, to run and protect wiring.

Most electricians start out by attending a technical school. Many technical schools offer programs related to safety and basic electrical information. Graduates usually receive credit toward their 4-year apprenticeship. Electricians may be required to take continuing education courses. These courses usually involve instruction related to safety practices, changes to the electrical code, and training from manufacturers in specific products.

Some electricians may start working independently, but sometimes they collaborate with others. For example, experienced electricians may work with building engineers and architects to help design electrical systems in new construction. Some electricians also may consult with other construction specialists, such as elevator installers and heating and air conditioning workers, to help install or maintain electrical or power systems. At larger companies, electricians are more likely to work as part of a crew; they may direct helpers and apprentices to complete jobs.

National Estimates

Minimum annual salary:	$30,420
Average annual salary:	$53,030
Maximum annual salary:	$82,930

The 3 industries that have the highest levels of employment in this profession are building equipment contractors, nonresidential building construction, and utility system construction.

Building equipment contractors pay their electricians an average hourly wage of $25.30 an hour. Utility system construction companies pay their electricians an average hourly wage of $25.16 an hour. Nonresidential building construction companies pay their electricians an average hourly wage of $25.13 an hour.

The following are the top paying industries for this profession:

Industry Hourly mean wage

Natural Gas Distribution	$36.26
Accounting, Tax Prep, Bookkeeping and Payroll Services	$35.20
Remediation and Other Waste Mgmt Services	$34.16

States with the most employed electricians:
1. Texas
2. California
3. New York
4. Florida
5. Illinois

Top paying states for this profession:
1. Alaska
2. New York
3. Illinois
4. Oregon
5. Hawaii

Brick / Block masons:

A brick or block mason is a person who builds and repairs walls, floors, partitions, fireplaces, chimneys, and other structures with brick or concrete block materials. Masons typically read blueprints, lay out foundations, mix mortar, clean excess mortar, and clean and polish surface with hand or power tools.

Although most masons learn through a formal apprenticeship, some learn informally on the job. Others learn through 1 or 2 year mason programs at technical colleges. For someone interested in becoming a mason, high school courses in English, math, mechanical drawing, and shop are useful.

National Estimates

Minimum annual salary:	$28,980
Average annual salary:	$50,370
Maximum annual salary:	$77,950

The 1 industry that has the highest levels of employment in this profession is foundation, structure, and building exterior contractors. These types of contractors pay their masons an average hourly wage of $23.51 an hour.

The following are the top paying industries for this profession:

Industry Hourly mean wage

Other Specialty Trade Contractors	$28.10
Nonresidential Building Construction	$27.84
Building Finishing Contractors	$26.80

States with the most employed masons:
1. New York
2. Texas
3. Ohio
4. California
5. Pennsylvania

Top paying states for this profession:
1. Massachusetts
2. New York
3. Hawaii
4. Illinois
5. New Jersey

Web developers:

A web developer is a person who design and create websites. They are responsible for the look of the site. They are also responsible for the site's technical aspects, such as performance and capacity, which are measures of a website's speed and how much traffic the site can handle. They also may create content for the site.

When creating a website, developers have to see their client's vision. They work with them to determine what sites should be used for, including ecommerce, news, or gaming. The developer has to decide which applications and designs will be appropriate.

Educational requirements for web developers vary with the setting they work in and the type of work they do. Requirements range from a high school diploma to a bachelor's degree. Web developers need to have a thorough understanding of HTML. Many employers also want developers to understand other languages, such as JavaScript or SQL, as well as have some knowledge of multimedia publishing tools, such as Flash. Throughout their career, web developers must keep up to date on new tools and computer languages.

National Estimates

Minimum annual salary:	$33,550
Average annual salary:	$66,100
Maximum annual salary:	$105,200

The 4 industries that have the highest levels of employment in this profession are computer systems design and related services, other information services, hosting services, and PR and advertising services.

Advertising and PR firms pay their developers an average hourly wage of $30.96 an hour. Hosting companies pay their developers an average hourly wage of $33.87 an hour. Other information service companies pay their developers an average hourly wage of $32.13 an hour. And computer system design companies pay their developers an average hourly wage of $32.20 an hour.

The following are the top paying industries for this profession:

Industry Hourly mean wage	
Securities and Commodity Contracts	$40.99
Intermediation and Brokerage Other Investment Pools and Funds	$40.92

States with the most employed web developers:
1. California
2. New York
3. Texas
4. Florida
5. Massachusetts

Top paying states for this profession:
1. District of Columbia
2. New York
3. Maryland
4. Virginia
5. Massachusetts

Insurance sales agents:

An insurance sales agent is a person who helps insurance companies generate new business by contacting potential customers and selling one or more types of insurance. The agent explains various insurance policies and helps clients choose plans that suit them.

Most employers require agents to have a high school diploma. Public speaking classes can be useful in improving sales techniques, and often agents will have taken courses in business, finance, or economics. Business knowledge is also helpful for sales agents hoping to advance to a managerial position.

Agents must be licensed in the states where they work. In most states, licenses are issued only to applicants who complete specified courses and who pass state exams covering insurance fundamentals and state insurance laws. Most state licensing authorities also require agents to take continuing education courses every 2 years, focusing on insurance laws, consumer protection, ethics, and the technical details of various insurance policies.

National Estimates

Minimum annual salary:	$26,120
Average annual salary:	$63,400
Maximum annual salary:	$116,940

The 3 industries that have the highest levels of employment in this profession are the agency and brokerage industry, insurance carriers, and travel arrangement and reservation services.

Insurance carriers pay their agents an average hourly wage of $30.71 an hour. Agencies and brokerages pay their agents an average hourly wage of $30.47 an hour. Travel arrangement and reservation service companies pay their agents an average hourly wage of $24.17 an hour.

The following are the top paying industries for this profession:

Industry Hourly mean wage

Insurance and Employee Benefit Funds	$37.16

States with the most employed insurance sales agents:

1. Texas
2. California
3 Florida
4. New York
5. Pennsylvania

Top paying states for this profession:
1. Rhode Island
2. Massachusetts
3. New York
4. California
5. Pennsylvania

Wholesale / Manufacturing sales rep:

A wholesale or manufacturing sales rep is a person who sells goods for wholesalers or manufacturers to businesses, government agencies, and other organizations. They contact customers, explain product features, answer any questions that their customers may have, and negotiate prices.

Educational requirements vary, depending on the type of product sold. If the products are not scientific or technical, a high school diploma is generally enough for entry into the occupation. Many sales representatives attend seminars in sales techniques or take courses in marketing, economics, communication, or even a foreign language to improve their ability to make sales.

Many companies have formal training programs for beginning wholesale and manufacturing sales representatives that last up to 1 year. Regardless of where they work, new employees may be trained by going along with experienced workers on their sales calls. As they gain familiarity with the firm's products and clients, the new workers gain more responsibility until they eventually get their own territory.

National Estimates

Minimum annual salary:	$37,720
Average annual salary:	$85,690
Maximum annual salary:	$147,320

The 1 industry that has the highest levels of employment in this profession is drug merchant wholesalers. Drug merchant wholesalers pay their reps an average hourly wage of $43.11 an hour.

The following are the top paying industries for this profession:

Industry Hourly mean wage	
Computer and Peripheral Equipment Manufacturing	$54.37

States with the most employed wholesale / manufacturing sales reps:
1. California
2. Texas
3. Florida
4. Ohio
5. Illinois

Top paying states for this profession:
1. Wyoming
2. New Hampshire
3. Nevada
4. Pennsylvania
5. Delaware

The Most Successful College Dropouts
1. Steve Jobs (Apple)
2. Bill Gates (Microsoft)
3. Paul Allen (Microsoft/Seattle Seahawks/Portland TrailBlazers)
4. Michael Dell (Dell)
5. Kevin Rose (Digg)
6. Shawn Fanning (Napster)
7. Evan Williams (Blogger/Twitter)
8. Matt Mullenweg (WordPress)

9. Arash Ferdowsi (Dropbox)
10. Aaron Levie (Box)
11. Mark Zuckerberg (Facebook)
12. Stacey Ferreira (MySocialCloud.com)
13. Dustin Moskovitz (Facebook/Asana)
14. Danielle Morrill (Twilio/Referly)
15. Jeffrey Kalmikoff (Threadless)
16. Zach Sims (Codecademy)
17. Sahil Lavingia (Pinterest/Gumroad)
18. Ben Milne (Dwolla)

CHAPTER 5

Go To College For Free

So, you want to go to college? You are not alone. Twenty-one million people go to college every year. A college degree has become almost a requirement for people to get priority consideration for a great career. Some people turn to higher education for a profitable career rather than a career that is profitable and satisfying.

While college offers a great variety of majors, more than half of them don't offer moderate income potential. The worst-paying majors tend to be in the arts, where the low pay is matched by its high unemployment rate (art major unemployment rate: 9%). The music, film, photography, theater, and fine arts industries all pay about a $30,000 starting salary to graduates. In some industries, it has become the new high school diploma for getting some of the lowest paying jobs. One example is the

Atlanta law firm, Slipakoff and Schuh, who requires a bachelor's degree for an in-house courier position that pays only $10 an hour.

As we have seen inflation affect the cost of living over the years, it has affected the cost of education too. Today, most hiring managers feel that people with high school diplomas are not as educated and capable of performing their jobs. They need the maturity and extra knowledge that a four year degree yields, which means that jobs that used to be reserved for baccalaureate graduates are now given to those with a master's degree. So, a student has to borrow tens of thousands of dollars to get the credentials only to spend the rest of their life trying to pay off the student debt. This reality doesn't inspire people to go to college.

The average cost of a bachelor's degree varies depending on the type of higher education institution and its prestige. It can range anywhere from $35,570 to $120,375. Anyone who graduates from college should be rewarded appropriately. Having a 4 year degree shows a degree of dedication. Moreover, a college education could be much more valuable if it was free. A tuition free degree can serve as additional empowerment to a student who lives in our struggling economy where the decrease in jobs has raised the qualification bar. They may not have to settle for a low paying job if they don't have to worry about student loan debt.

Thankfully, there are programs that grant people the opportunity to study for free. Most of these programs will pay for tuition costs only, which leaves you responsible for the miscellaneous fees. However, there are a few programs that pay for everything. Some of these programs are open to general public while others are reserved to particular people.

Full Scholarships

Indiana University @ Bloomington

Cox Research Scholars Program

- *Must have a minimum SAT score of 1360 or ACT score of 31 and rank in the top 5% of their graduating class*
- *Must maintain a cumulative GPA of 3.0 if accepted*

Kelley Scholars Program

- *Must have a minimum SAT score of 1350 or ACT score of 32, along with a 3.8 GPA*
- *Must maintain a 3.5 GPA among other requirements if accepted*

Truman State University

General John Pershing Scholarship

- *Must be in the top 3% of their HS class with SAT or ACT scores that are in the top 3% nationally*

Truman Leadership Scholarship

- *Must be a Missouri resident and be in the top 3% of their HS class with SAT or ACT scores that are in the top 3% nationally*

University of Kentucky

Otis A. Singletary Scholarship

- *Must have a minimum SAT score of 1360 or ACT score of 31 with a 3.5 GPA*

Presidential Scholarship

- *Must have a minimum SAT score of 1360 or ACT score of 31 with a 3.5 GPA*

Patterson Scholarship
- *No scholarship application required*

University of Akron
Akron Public Schools Innovation Generation Scholarship
- *Students enrolled in Akron public schools who apply for admission are automatically considered for the scholarship*
- *Some APS seniors will be promised a tuition-free college degree*

Honors Scholarship
- *Every student admitted to University of Akron who applies for admission prior to the honors deadline is considered for an honors scholarship. First consideration is given those who meet the following criteria: minimum GPA of 3.5, highest 10% class rank, minimum score of 27 for ACT and 1800 for SAT.*
- *Some honors scholarships will cover the full tuition costs and fees.*

Pacific Union College
National Merit / Achievement Scholarship
- *These awards are given to freshmen who achieve a high score on the PSATs*
- *Scholarships are renewable to students who maintain a 3.5 GPA*

Lorain County Community College
Trustee Scholarship
- *No application is required for students attending a Lorain County high school*
- *New Lorain County high school grads who earn a minimum 3.7 GPA at the end of their 6th semester high school grading period*

- *Recipients must earn a minimum 2.5 LCCC cumulative GPA each semester to maintain scholarship eligibility*

Choose Ohio First Scholarship

- *LCCC students must have a 3.0 high school or college GPA, resides in Ohio, declared a STEM major, and register for a minimum of 8 credit hours.*
- *To be eligible for renewal, students must maintain a cumulative GPA of at least 3.0 and make sufficient progress toward degree completion in a timely manner*

Diversity Incentive Award

- *New Lorain County high school grads who earn a minimum 2.5 high school GPA by the end of the 6th semester high school grading period and are of African American, Hispanic, Pacific Island, Middle Eastern, Native American, Indian or Asian descent*
- *The award will cover 3 years or 72 credits*
- *Each recipient must enroll at LCCC on a full-time basis and work a job either on or off campus. Recipients must earn a minimum cumulative GPA of 2.0 each semester to maintain award eligibility*

The College of St. Scholastica

CSS Yes Scholarship

- *Must have a 3.0 GPA, a minimum ACT score of 20, be an U.S. citizen and Minnesota resident*
- *To be eligible for renewal, students must maintain a 2.4 GPA*

State of Minnesota

If you are a Minnesota ward in an undergraduate program and under the age of 21, you may attend post-secondary schools tuition-free.

Internships
City Vision College
- *Free tuition for a full year of college paid by the hosting ministry as a part of a 29 hour week internship*
- *Housing is provided by the hosting ministry (or a cash equivalent living stipend)*
- *Any Pell grant or federal financial aid is paid as cash payment to the student (up to $5,645)*
- *May be extended yearly upon mutual agreement*
- *Must be at least 18 years old, a U.S. citizen / national / permanent resident / have a student or work visa, a Christian, and have a high school diploma or GED*
- *Must be able to make a 1 year commitment and able to financially live on just free housing (and any outside income sources you have)*
- *Able to relocate to a site ministry location (unless a site exists at your current location)*

Bakke Graduate University
- *Free tuition in Bakke Graduate University paid by the host ministry as a part of a 29 hour week internship*
- *Housing is provided by the hosting ministry (or a cash equivalent living stipend)*
- *Must be at least 18 years old, a U.S. or Canadian citizen / national / permanent resident / have a student or work visa, a Christian, and have a high school diploma or GED*
- *Must have a bachelor's or master's degree from an accredited institution and at least 5 years experience for doctorate level programs*
- *Able to relocate to a site ministry location (unless a site exists at your current location)*

- *Must be able to complete the program (minimum of 2 years depending on academic load taken)*

Sponsored Programs

The Power Of You program

- *Covers students' tuition and fees for 2 years or up to 72 credits at Minneapolis Community and Technical College or at St. Paul College*
- *Must have graduated from a public, alternative, charter, or partner expansion high schools in the Twin Cities*
- *Must meet the criteria to apply for FAFSA*
- *Must meet the family adjusted gross income cap of $75,000*
- *Take the assessment tests and score above ABE in 2 or more placements*

Kalamazoo Promise

- *To provide each Kalamazoo Public Schools graduate with the opportunity to attend college with up to a full scholarship.*
- *Must be a student who graduated from a Kalamazoo Public School, are residing in the district, and have been a KPS student for 4 years or more.*
- *Must be admitted to and enrolled at any public State of Michigan university or community college*
- *Must maintain a 2.0 grade point average at the post-secondary institution*
- *Complete a minimum of 12 credit hours per semester*

Oklahoma's Promise

- *Pays full tuition at public universities and portion of tuition at private universities*
- *Must be a student residing in Oklahoma*

- *Must be a U.S. citizen or lawfully present in the U.S.*
- *Must have a household federal adjusted gross income that doesn't exceed $100,000*
- *Must have at least a 2.0 GPA for courses taken during the sophomore semester and at least a 2.5 GPA for courses taken during the junior semester and thereafter*

Tulsa Achieves

- *Provides up to 100 percent of tuition and fees to graduating seniors, living in Tulsa County, who enroll at Tulsa Community College the fall after they graduate*
- *Must reside in Tulsa County while in high school and maintain Tulsa County residency while in the program*
- *Must apply to Tulsa Achieves as a high school senior*
- *Must graduate from a public or private high school, or home school with at least a 2.0 GPA on a 4.0 scale*
- *Must be a U.S. citizen or legal resident of the U.S.*
- *Must maintain good academic standing (earn at least a 1.7 GPA with 30 attempted credit hours and at least a 2.0 with 31 attempted credit hours or more)*
- *Must complete 40 hours of volunteer service each academic year*

Household Income

Soka University of America

Soka Opportunity Scholarship

- *All admitted students to the BA in Liberal Arts program whose annual earned family income is $60,000 or less, and who have neither graduated from college, will receive free tuition*
- *Must obtain a cumulative or term 3.0 GPA to renew this scholarship on an annual basis*

Global Merit Scholarship

- *The top students of each entering class will be considered for this scholarship and all admitted students are given equal and automatic consideration for this award*
- *This scholarship covers the entire "Cost of Attendance" which includes not only the costs of tuition, room, and board but also costs like travel, personal expenses, books and supplies.*

Washington and Lee University

Johnson Scholarship

- *Winners of this scholarship receive free tuition, room, and board*
- *Johnson scholars also receive $7000 in additional funding to support their summer experiences (internships, volunteer experiences or research projects)*

Albemarle Corporation Honor Scholarship

- *For entering students with an interest in chemistry, chemistry engineering or business related to the petrochemical or chemical industry*
- *This scholarship is renewable if the student maintains a 3.3 GPA*

Gilreath Honor Scholarship

- *For entering students with an exemplary academic and extracurricular record, coupled with an interest in chemistry*
- *This scholarship is renewable if the student maintains a 3.3 GPA*

Keelty Honor Scholarship

- *For students from the Baltimore area who are financially unable to attend Washington and Lee University without assistance*
- *This scholarship is renewable if the student maintains a 3.3 GPA*

Max and Sylvia Weinstein Scholarship
- *For entering students of the Jewish faith with an exemplary academic and extracurricular record*
- *This scholarship is renewable if the student maintains a 3.3 GPA*

Dallas Alumni Honor Scholarship
- *For entering students from the Dallas area*
- *This scholarship is renewable if the student maintains a 3.3 GPA and satisfactory personal performance (i.e. extracurricular activities and community service)*

Native American roots
Michigan's Native American tuition waiver program (state residents who have reside in Michigan at least a year, are 25% Native American and enrolled in a federally recognized tribe are waived from any tuition obligations at any 2 or 4 year public in-state institution)

9/11 Victims
Massachusetts and Connecticut provide private memorial scholarships to dependents of 9/11 victims as well as the federal government offers immediate loan forgiveness.

Natural Disaster Victims
Minnesota grants tuition waivers to students who have survived a substantial natural disaster.

Medicaid Recipients
Michigan residents who have had at least 2 years of Medicaid coverage, may be eligible for full tuition at in-state 2 year public institutions or up to $2000 at in-state 4 year public institutions. Students must enroll within 4 years from their high school graduation to qualify.

University Employee Benefits

Any employee (excluding temporary and hourly employees) at the University of Washington is exempt from paying tuition as long as he/she remains as an employee.

Any employee at the University of Cincinnati is exempt from paying tuition as long as he/she remains as an employee. This benefit is extended to their spouse (or domestic partner) and children.

Any employee at Owens Community College is exempt from paying tuition as long as he/she remains as an employee. This benefit is extended to their spouse.

State Employees Benefits

Most state employees that fall under the civil service sector are exempt from paying tuition at the University of Washington as long as he/she remains as a state employee.

Veterans

Benedictine University (3 years of free tuition to veterans and other benefits may apply depending on their situation)

University of Rochester (full scholarships to veterans who served at least 3 years of service)

University of Wyoming (10 semesters of free tuition to veterans and their surviving dependents)

Unemployed

An unmarried, independent student with no income will most likely qualify for the maximum $5,550 in Pell Grant funds for the school year and may qualify for up to an additional $4,000 Supplemental Educational Opportunity Grant from the federal government. With the low tuition costs of community colleges, students can study tuition-free with only a Pell Grant at most community colleges.

New Jersey offers a full tuition waiver at in-state public institutions for residents who have been out of a job for at least three years.

Benedictine University (full scholarship to undergraduate students who have been unemployed for 18 months)

Tuition-Free Colleges

- Alice Lloyd College (as long as they work 10 hours a week and must live in KY, OH, TN, VA, or WV)
- Barclay College (must be a full-time student)
- Berea College (as long as they work 10 hours a week and only applies to students from low income families)
- College of the Ozarks (as long as they work 15 hours a week)
- Curtis Institute of Music
- Deep Springs College (students must work on the school's cattle ranch and alfalfa farm)
- Macaulay Honors College (4 year scholarship, laptop, and $7500 to pursue study abroad programs and internships)
- Saint Louis Christian College (must be an on campus full-time student)
- United States Air Force Academy (Postgraduate service is required)
- United States Coast Guard Academy (Postgraduate service is required)
- United States Merchant Marine Academy
- United States Military (Army) Academy (Postgraduate service is required and students must play on a sports team each semester)
- United States Naval Academy (Postgraduate service is required)
- Webb Institute

Study Abroad

<u>Germany</u>

- Free University of Berlin
- Goethe University (most degree programs are tuition-free)
- Friedrich Schiller University of Jena
- Friedrich-Alexander University (the official language of FAU is German. Sufficient knowledge of the language is necessary)

<u>Norway</u>

Norwegian University of Life Sciences

- Norwegian University of Science and Technology
- University of Agder
- University of Bergen
- University of Nordland
- University of Oslo
- University of Stavanger
- University of Tromso

<u>Finland</u>

- Åbo Akademi University
- University of Helsinki (most degree programs are tuition-free)
- University of Jyväskylä
- University of Eastern Finland
- University of Lapland
- University of Tampere
- Helsinki University of Technology
- Lappeenranta University of Technology
- Tampere University of Technology

CHAPTER 6

Graduate With A
Bachelor's Degree In 1 Year

A lot of students have been accustomed to spending four years in college to get a bachelor's degree. Academic professionals, employers, mainstream media, and parents claim that it is the best investment that one can make to ensure a prosperous future ahead. As we have seen in the previous chapters, this is not always true.

Four years is a big commitment. Almost 40% of students who enter college graduate within 4 years while almost 60% of students graduate within 6 years, according to the Department of Education. Many students try to balance work and school during these times. They feel the necessity to work due to a lack of financial support from their parents or student aid. According to an American Council on Education study, 42% of students work more than 20 hours per week. The financial support factor makes a big difference in their college choices as well. 62% chose their college based on proximity to home or work and 54% based on a convenient class schedule, according to a Bill and Melinda Gates funded study called "With Their Whole Lives Ahead of Them."

Students may delay graduation for a number of reasons. For students who choose to take on an internship, it can be tough to fit in all of their necessary courses for that semester. Sometimes, overcrowded classes can make it impossible for students to take the necessary courses to graduate on time (even one unavailable prerequisite can cost a student an entire year). This very reason forces students to take unnecessary courses that are unlikely to fulfill their degree requirements. Another common reason is when students decide to change their major which usually postpones their initial graduation date.

The growing illusion of the 4 year degree has prompted a number of colleges to entice students with a 4 year guarantee or else, the extra tuition will be free. The University of Buffalo, California State University, University of Nebraska, Juniata College, University of Minnesota, and Pace University are some of the colleges that have 4 year guarantee programs in place. One thing to note is that the most generous of guarantees only cover tuition after the 4th year, which still leaves students to pay for room and board costs and miscellaneous school related fees (i.e. student activity fee, cost of books, lab fee, etc). There are also colleges like Ball State University, who offer incentives rather than guarantees. Ball State started paying $500 to students who graduated on time last year.

There are a few colleges who take pride in ensuring that students graduate on time and they have the stats to prove it. Carleton College, Williams College, Bowdoin College, and Columbia University all boast 4 year graduation rates of at least 90% of their students. So, what are these schools doing that others are not? I think there are two factors that can explain it. One factor is that these colleges tend to be highly selective which may help them select the brightest students (who are usually known to be the most driven and determined). The other factor is that they all have small undergraduate classes (none of them enrolls more than 10,000 students). Their size often allows for more personal attention from teachers and administrators, which can help students stay on course.

If most colleges are more interested in their profit margins and less interested in the welfare of the student, can it be the very reason of why students are dropping out of college?

From the same Bill and Melinda Gates study mentioned early in this chapter, 21% of students who dropped out of college stated that they needed a break. As mentioned previously, 4 years is a big commitment. I can't imagine myself going back to college for 4 more years. Most employers tend to hire college grads over high school grads because they usually associate a college degree with a person's dedication. Several years of work experience also shows dedication just as much as a person with a college degree. Usually, the applicants that have both are very likely to get the job.

31% of students who dropped out of college stated that the cost of attendance was not affordable. 58% of college dropouts stated that they had no help from their parents while 69% stated they had no scholarships or loans to help cover the costs. When the average annual cost of a bachelor's degree is $60,000 (if the student graduates in 4 years), how can college be affordable to the poor and middle class person? The $60,000 price tag is not entirely accurate when you consider that the majority of students never graduate in 4 years. It can cost much more depending on the school.

35% of students who dropped out of college stated that balancing work and school was too stressful. If students were given academic curriculums that focused only on courses pertaining to their major, students wouldn't feel as stressed in balancing work and school because they would be in school for 2 years instead of 4 years.

The students in the study were asked to suggest some solutions that would increase graduation rates. Their first suggestion was to allow part-time students to qualify for student aid. I think this is very important for it applies mostly to single parents or low income households. Most of them live below, at, or slightly above the poverty line and find it difficult to pay for their own tuition.

Their second suggestion was to provide more flexible weekend and evening classes. This problem becomes one of the main deterrents for people who are considering college. We live in a society that depends on convenience. Most of these schools make tens to hundreds of millions every year. It would actually be in their best interest to be more flexible since it encourages more people to enroll in their schools.

Their third suggestion was to cut college costs. This suggestion alone would be a great way to motivate more people to go to college. There are other ways that they can address this concern like sliding scale tuition. I have always been a big supporter of this idea. Anyone who meets or exceeds a designated household income level will pay the regular tuition costs. Anyone else who has an income below the designated income level will pay an adjusted rate based on their income.

If you don't want to spend 4 years in college, I completely understand. I'm going to show you how you can get a bachelor's degree in 1 year. You will pay a fraction of the cost and have your degree completed in a fraction of the time.

Too many students are only aware of the traditional path to obtaining a college degree. They pick up a college course book and see all of the degree programs that are available. They pick a major and start working on meeting their degree requirements for the next few years. This is the only way that is known to them.

We all know that the credits are what ultimately deliver us the college degree. Your credit requirements may differ depending on the type of degree (usually 60 credits for an associate's degree and 120 for a bachelor's degree). There are 2 ways to earn credits by taking classes at higher education institutions (community colleges, 4 year public or private universities) and earning credits by examination.

Credit by examination refers to college level tests on certain subjects. The College Level Examination Program (CLEP) and Dante's Subject Standardized Tests (DSST) are the most popular. So, how does it work? It's quite simple actually. You take a test covering an entire subject (like business, psychology or accounting), pass the exam, and you earn the credits. The best part about credit by examination is that you pay a fraction of the cost (usually $80 per test) in a fraction of the time (in as little as 2 weeks). Although CLEP and DSST do not offer degrees, you can transfer the credits to an accredited college or university to be awarded a degree.

There is also lesser known credit by examinations providers like StraighterLine, TestDriveCollege, and Propero. They typically offer courses that are not usually offered by CLEP, DSST, GRE, UExcel (formerly known as ECE), and TECEP.

Most universities and colleges have strict residency requirements which mean that they will only accept a portion of your credits from CLEP and DSST exams. However, there are 3 schools that offer an easy residency requirement. Excelsior College, Thomas Edison State College, and Charter Oak State College will accept all of your credits from CLEP and DSST exams if you take their capstone course. SUNY Empire State College will accept 75% of your credits for their bachelor's degree program.

Any of the mentioned colleges offer these core benefits: regional accreditation accept 100% of your credits for transfer, and credit by examination course offerings. However, there are some differences between the 3 schools.

Excelsior College offers the largest section of credit by examination options in the UExcel program. The UExcel exams are available at Pearson Vue test centers.

Thomas Edison State College costs and credit equivalency programs (TECEP) are somewhat similar to Excelsior but their tests are done by paper and pencil instead of it being computer based.

Charter Oak State College is similar to the other two schools and still accept GRE subject tests. You can also register for ECE's through Charter Oak. It is currently the most inexpensive when compared to the other 2 schools and offers a tuition payment plan.

Thomas Edison and Charter Oak are state funded. So, they are the schools to consider if you're interested in obtaining financial aid. Any of the other schools or course providers mentioned in this chapter may offer payment plans but unlikely to offer financial aid.

So, what would be the typical cost of a college degree via CLEP and DSST exams? The cost of the exams would be about $3,000 for 120 credits plus $1500 to transfer them to Excelsior. If you included the cost of CLEP exam books and/or study guides, you should pay no more than $5000 total. You may be able to borrow the exam books or study guides from your public library to cut down on your costs.

Credit by examination is not for everybody. Before pursuing credit by exam, students should consider whether they would be better served taking the class formally. Some students crave interaction with their classmates and certain skills (i.e. public speaking and critical thinking) that would be missed if they test out of a course. However, if you are a good test taker, then credit by examination may be the right option for you.

Please keep in mind that credit by examination is not as difficult as one may think. These types of exams are multiple choice, which should make it easier for anyone. I'll take this opportunity to offer some helpful tips that can really make the difference for someone who is taking these types of exams.

Tips for Success in CLEP/DSST/UExcel/TECEP exams

1. *Process of Elimination.* Usually these tests offer 4 answers. If you can eliminate at least 1 choice, you've just increased your chances to 33%. Eliminate 2 choices and it's 50%.

2. *Clarity of Question.* Read the question and understand what the question is asking of you. Incorrect answers are often chosen because the reader doesn't understand the question.

3. *Look for similar questions.* Sometimes, a previous question is reworded differently. By correctly answering 1 question, you may be able to answer those similar questions correctly or at least eliminate the incorrect answers.

4. *Adverbs = your friends.* When questions contain adverbs (i.e. always, usually, never, except), they usually hint to the answer just by the very nature of the word.

5. *Trust your instincts.* Don't change the answer that you originally suspected unless you're sure that it's incorrect.

6. *Answer every question.* There is no penalty for guessing. You are better off guessing the answer. After all, you may get it right. Don't you want to increase your chances of passing the test?

There is also an option called portfolio credit. This method requires that you demonstrate a skill that is equivalent to a college course. For example, you may have written a stellar budget report that could be used to earn you credits for an accounting course. The thing to remember is making sure the competency for which you're requesting credit has a correlation to some accredited college course.

The average person could earn their bachelor's degree in 1 year. If you are an overachiever or just don't have a lot of patience, it is quite possible to earn your bachelor's degree in 6 months. If you wanted to get your degree solely through credit by examination, your choice of majors will be limited. Liberal arts, business, psychology, sociology, information technology, and criminal justice are the most common majors but there are other majors offered depending on the school.

I'm going to show you the necessary requirements for a person to get a bachelor's degree in liberal arts via examinations in 1 year.

1 CLEP or DSST exam = $80 per exam / U = Upper Level Course	
CLEP: College Composition	(6 credits)
CLEP: Humanities	(6 credits)
CLEP: Social Sciences and History	(6 credits)
CLEP: American Government	(3 credits)
CLEP: College Algebra	(3 credits)
CLEP: Natural Sciences	(6 credits)
CLEP: Principles of Macroeconomics	(3 credits)
CLEP: Principles of Microeconomics	(3 credits)
CLEP: Financial Accounting	(3 credits)
CLEP: Introductory Business Law	(3 credits)
CLEP: Principles of Management	(3 credits)
CLEP: Principles of Marketing	(3 credits)
CLEP: Intro to Educational Psychology	(3 credits)
CLEP: Analyzing and Interpreting Literature	(6 credits)
CLEP: Human Growth and Development	(3 credits)
CLEP: Biology	(6 credits)
CLEP: Spanish I	(6 credits)
CLEP: Spanish II	(12 credits)
DSST: Principles of Public Speaking	(3 credits)

DSST: Business Ethics and Society	(3 credits) U
DSST: Intro to World Religions	(3 credits) U
DSST: Business Law II	(3 credits) U
DSST: Principles of Supervision	(3 credits)
DSST: Environment and Humanity	(3 credits)
DSST: Lifespan Development Psychology	(3 credits)
DSST: Rise and Fall of the Soviet Union	(3 credits) U
DSST: Here's To Your Health	(3 credits) U
DSST: Principles of Finance	(3 credits) U
DSST: Management Information Systems	(3 credits) U
DSST: Substance Abuse	(3 credits) U
DSST: The Civil War and Reconstruction	(3 credits) U
DSST: Ethics in America	(3 credits) U

Note: CLEP courses are typically known as "lower level" courses while DSST courses are known to have both "lower and upper level" courses. Most schools will require you to have at least 30 upper level courses prior to graduation.

Excelsior's UExcel exam = fees vary	
SCIX-259: Science of Nutrition	(3 credits) $95
LA-498: Liberal Arts Capstone	(3 credits) U $1275
IN-102: Information Literacy	(1 credit) U $425

So, if you followed this course guide, you could easily have your bachelor's degree in a year. I have included 3 extra lower level courses to give you some other course choices. You can go to clep.collegeboard.org to find the full list of CLEP exams and getcollegecredit.com to find the full list of DSST exams. This plan would require you to take a total of 32 exams in 1 year (or 8 exams every quarter). Most of the CLEP and

DSST exams are not very difficult to pass but there are study guides available to assure you the best chances of success.

If you were to transfer all of your credits to Excelsior to obtain a degree, this would be the items on your cost sheet.

CLEP and/or DSST exams: $80 per exam x 32 exams =	$2650.00
Admissions Fee	$ 80.00
Enrollment Fee (Multi-source option)	$1065.00
Tuition (@ Excelsior): $425 per credit x 4 credits =	$1700.00
Annual Student Fee	$495.00
Graduation Fee	$ 495.00
Estimated Total Cost:	*$6485.00

This total does not include the cost of study materials or other fees (like administrative fees). Prices may vary for study materials. You may opt to buy the study guides from the Collegeboard and DSST website, Amazon, or from a test prep sites like InstantCert Academy or iStudySmart. It is also possible to borrow some of these study guides from your local public library. Most test centers charge a non-refundable administration fee to facilitate these exams.

CHAPTER 7

Change Careers Without Going Back To College

Are you stuck in a job to only pay your bills and/or take care of your family? Are you ready for a career change because you're unfulfilled with your current career?

"People are holding on to their jobs not because they want to, but because they don't have much opportunity as they once did" says Anthony Carnevale, director of Georgetown University Center on Education and Workforce. The truth is employees sticking with the same job longer today than they did 10, 20, and 30 years ago and that's not necessarily a good thing. Rosemary Haefner, vice president of HR for CareerBuilder, suspects that "fewer people have voluntarily left jobs because the chances of finding a new or better one were low compared to a healthier economic cycle."

Only 14 percent of Americans believe that they have the perfect job and more than half want to change careers, according to Reuters. A University of Phoenix's study has shown that the most coveted jobs are in the arts and sciences, healthcare, technology, and business management. I bet your dream career is probably listed in one of those industries.

Hope is not lost. You don't have to be stuck in your job any longer. There are several ways that can transition you into a new career smoothly. No need to worry about jeopardizing your current job. No need to worry about going back to college either.

The first way to switch careers successfully is through internships. We have always known internships to be associated with college. Usually, juniors and seniors will do an internship to gain real world experience that will be complementary to their college education. This is helpful because a lot of employers won't hire a college grad without relevant work experience. What's interesting is that all internships don't require a person to be enrolled in a higher education institution. There is no law that requires companies to hire only college students and graduates.

Idealist.org is a website that you can find internship opportunities offered by non-profit organizations. They have hundreds of internship opportunities listed in different fields like education, community development, agriculture, human services among others. Internships. com is another site that you can find internships from for profit and non-profit organizations. The opportunities are not as plentiful as idealist.org but it is still one of the more commonly known websites for internships.

LinkedIn is now known as the best website for internship opportunities. It started off out as a social networking site for business and has expanded to other areas. LinkedIn has millions of registered businesses that provide thousands of internship opportunities. They have the widest selection of opportunities, offering internships in 10+ industries.

One company that is leading the way in unique internships is Wholesome Homes. Wholesome Homes is a Michigan based real estate company that offers virtual internships through internships.com and LinkedIn. They typically offer marketing, communications, real estate, human resources, and business internships.

The only applicant requirement is that they are at least 18 years old and demonstrates a strong interest in one of their internships. They are quite likely to match their interns with a career if they delivered a superb performance as an intern. Google, Sallie Mae, VH1, and Sony are a few companies that have hired their interns based on their relationship with their contacts in those companies.

Sometimes, there are opportunities that go unnoticed because they are not advertised. You can learn more about these opportunities by plugging into your network. There are a lot of employers that will hire an applicant who is a friend of a friend or who is recommended by a respectable work professional. While that applicant's credentials may play a factor, it's usually not the primary factor.

There's an old adage that says "your network is your net worth." That adage still holds true to this day. LinkedIn is a good website to develop your network. You can find connections by utilizing your current social media profiles (Facebook friends, Twitter followers, etc) and then by connecting with people in their networks. Networking locally is always good, whether it's through conferences, symposiums, or meetup groups. However, LinkedIn may be the faster way.

The second way to switch careers successfully is through volunteering. Volunteering has always been a noble thing. There are so many causes that inspire a person to volunteer but overall it is to contribute to a person, community, or social issue. There are various volunteer opportunities that have different time commitments. Some of them require that you dedicate yourself on a full-time basis while others only require a part-time commitment.

One way to volunteer is through AmeriCorps. AmeriCorps offer multiple full-time, part-time, and summer only volunteer opportunities nationwide in different fields. Some of these fields are community outreach, disaster relief, education, health, public safety, technology as well as several others. It is a great way to gain new skills in a field that you're hoping to turn into a career.

Part-time AmeriCorps opportunities typically offer a living allowance and a completion stipend or an education award. The part-time option is probably a better fit for those who have full-time jobs and/or other important commitments. The full-time AmeriCorps opportunities provide a bigger living allowance and stipend or education award than part-timers. If you are a college student that is considering doing a gap year or you simply can afford to do it, then AmeriCorps may be a good option for you.

Another way to volunteer is through the Mercy Volunteers Corps. This niche opportunity is somewhat similar to the AmeriCorps format but it focuses only in the areas of education, healthcare, and social services. It is offered in 10 U.S. cities and requires a 1 year, full-time commitment. Mercy Volunteers receive housing, health insurance, transportation, food and personal stipends, and student loan deferment (depending on the lender). Mercy volunteers at most U.S. service sites are eligible for a $5,500 education award at the completion of their service year.

Any of these volunteer opportunities are good ways to gain experience in your desired field prior to making the official career change. After your stint with one of these volunteer programs, it should be much easier for you to land a career in that field since you'll have some relevant qualifications under your belt.

The third way to switch careers successfully is through Teach For America. This is a great option if you are strongly considering a career as a teacher. The only requirement is to be a U.S. citizen or national/

permanent resident, have a bachelor's degree from an accredited college or university, and a cumulative 2.5 GPA. You will get a starting teacher's salary that varies between $31,000 - $50,000 (depending on the region), a $5,000 AmeriCorps education award, the possibility of earning a master's degree part-time, and health insurance.

The fourth way to switch careers successfully is through online education. There are education providers that teach you skills depending on your interest.

The Khan Academy is a non-profit organization that provides free world class education material to anyone, anywhere. Their course library offers courses in math (from 3rd grade to the collegiate level), science, economics, finance, humanities, and others.

The Open CourseWare Consortium is a global community of higher education institutions that offers free educational resources in a course format. Their course catalog offers courses in computer science, geography, health, history, religion, social sciences among others.

Lynda.com provides training videos with subscription plans that range from $25 a month up to $250 a year, which can help you learn about business, design, video, music production, computing, and other skills.

So, from what we covered, it is not necessary to go back to college to learn and start a new career. Some of these options may be a better fit for you than others, depending on your personal situation. You probably will need to go back for a specialized profession if you want to be a doctor or a lawyer. However, for most non-specialized professions, one of these 4 options will work for you.

CHAPTER 8

Get Paid To Support a Charitable Cause

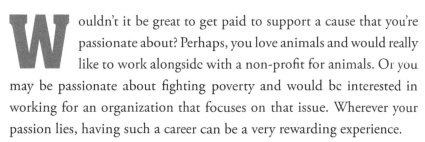

Wouldn't it be great to get paid to support a cause that you're passionate about? Perhaps, you love animals and would really like to work alongside with a non-profit for animals. Or you may be passionate about fighting poverty and would be interested in working for an organization that focuses on that issue. Wherever your passion lies, having such a career can be a very rewarding experience.

Some people are happy with a white collar, corporate career. Some people are fine with a blue collar career. However, you may be a person who doesn't care as much about either but more about coming to work every day with the intent in making a difference that will benefit society. If this is true, you are likely to prefer a career in the non-profit industry than any other industry.

So, a non-profit career may be the right fit for you. How do you know for sure? Perhaps, you don't. While passion is important when considering a career, passion alone is not enough nor does it assure that you will be successful in that career. I can be really passionate about playing professional basketball but it doesn't mean that I'll do well in making it to play on that level. I think it's important that we are realistic about our goals. Being realistic about our goals and setting them up properly (the MTO way) will assure that we will be successful.

Working at a non-profit can be fulfilling and stressful at the same time. Employees there have to stay hopeful about the organization's goals, even when success appears to be out of reach. The work environment can be frustrating when employees are expected to do more work with fewer resources and create miracles on a regular basis. The constant focus on fundraising can cause internal issues to get ignored, which may become a bigger problem during a crisis.

Working at a non-profit can also be a very rewarding experience from a personal and professional standpoint. The opportunities for growth are endless. In a for-profit company, it is likely that 3 corporate employees are assigned to 1 project. In a non-profit, it is likely that 3 projects are assigned to 1 employee. These employees can learn new skill sets faster, which can lead to faster career development and more diverse job responsibilities.

So, what do non-profits look for in employees? Laura Otting (founder and president of the Nonprofit Professionals Advisory Group), offers the following advice: "Non-profits are looking for people who have a strong track record of leadership and the ability to influence their constituencies. They need to work with partners, funders, and friends in the community and manage those relationships well. Non-profits seek employees who are good at delegating kindness and empathy, while simultaneously demanding accountability. Recognize that people volunteer and serve with different non-profit groups for different reasons. Strong leaders know how to bring out the best in everyone and how to leverage all available talents."

For those people who are on the fence about entering the non-profit world, Laura Otting says that "working for a non-profit is like starting a marathon. You have to be committed long-term, even when the finish line is out of sight. A track record of dedication to the cause or constituency demonstrates an authentic commitment, and this commitment shows your future nonprofit employer that you will take their marathon seriously."

Another tip worth noting is that hiring managers are likely to give priority to candidates who have had volunteer experience. After all, it is hard for a candidate to profess that they care about the organization's mission when they have no relevant experience to back up their claims.

In today's society, non-profit employment opportunities are numerous. According to the 2013 Nonprofit Employment Trends Survey, job opportunities tend to be greater in areas dealing with health, faith, education, environment, and animals.

So, where can you look for non-profit careers? You can find them on the big job board sites like Indeed, CareerBuilder, SimplyHired, and LinkedIn. All of those websites post job listings from non-profits. However, you may have to use filters to separate them from the other job listings. You can also find them on niche sites like Encore.org, Idealist.org, The Bridgespan Group, CommonGood Careers, The Foundation Center, The NonProfit Times, and The Chronicle of Philanthropy. These niche sites are usually better when looking for non-profit career opportunities.

Many nonprofits operate on a different salary scale than traditional corporate organizations. However, there are several non-profit careers that will guarantee you a higher paying salary.

A **grant coordinator** is a person who keeps the money coming to the nonprofits. They typically figure out which grants are best for the organization, develop proposals and follow up when necessary to ensure everyone is in compliance with the grant requirements. The grant coordinator is commonly referred to as the overseer of the grant procurement process. The median annual salary for a grant coordinator is *$51,000.

A **program officer** is a person who figures out the who, what, and how of giving out grant money. They have to assure that the right grant gets to the right organization. Nonprofits hire them because for their deep knowledge and expertise in a particular area. The median annual salary for a program officer is *$60,000.

A **communications director** is a person who is responsible for a nonprofit's public relations and media outreach. They usually manage PR staff, create communication strategies, and serve as the spokesperson for the organization. It is up to the communications director to assure that the organization has a good standing with the public. The median annual salary for a communications director is *$63,000.

A **director of development** is a person who is responsible for the necessary fundraising that a nonprofit needs to continue its existence. They create fundraising strategies and oversee outreach to major funding sources like grants, corporate investors, individual donors, and fundraising events. In some nonprofits, a director of development will also serve as the grant coordinator. The median annual salary for a director of development is *$58,000.

An **executive director** is a person that is commonly recognized as the CEO in a non-profit organization. They are the leaders and visionaries behind their mission statement and the core values of the organization. The executive director is the skipper of the ship. Their actions are what will determine the success or failure of the organization's efforts. The median annual salary for an executive director is *$61,000.

Salary stats provided by Salary.com, Payscale, and GlassDoor

The Huffington Post released a survey in 2012 about the top 10 non-profits to work for. The following factors were used to create the list rankings: leadership and planning, corporate culture and communication, role satisfaction, work environment, relationship with supervisor, training and development, pay and benefits, and overall employee engagement.

The Top 10 Non-Profit Organizations to Work For
1. Wounded Warrior Project
2. Brighton Center
3. DoSomething.org
4. SightLife
5. Alzheimer's Association
6. Grand Rapids Community Foundation
7. New Jersey Society of Certified Public Accountants
8. Animal Legal Defense Fund
9. Natural Resources Defense Council
10. Make-A-Wish Metro and Western New York

CNN did a story last year discussing the worst charities in America. The worst charity in America is the Kids Wish Network. Every year, they are known to raise millions of dollars in donations for dying children and their families. The Center for Investigative Reporting has found that less than 3% of their total donations actually go towards helping kids. The majority of the remaining funds are used to enrich the charity's operators and the for-profit companies that the charity hires to extract more donations.

CIR has also found that the 50 worst charities in America devote less than 4% of donations raised to people in need. Most of these charity operators have taken multiple salaries, arrange fundraising contracts with friends, and lied to donors about the distribution of the money.

Are These Charities Truly Paying The Price?

- More than 35 charities and their hired solicitors have been caught breaking the rules multiple times and continue to take money from donors. The most frequent violators have been cited 5+ times.
- 39 of those charities have been disciplined by state regulators.

HOWEVER

States typically issue a small fine. The most common penalty is $500, a small price for organizations that collect millions.

- 8 of those charities have been banned in at least 1 state.

HOWEVER

Those same charities continue raising donations elsewhere.

State regulators also make it easy for operators to start over. Instead of targeting individuals, they often only ban the charity which allows executives to move to another organization.

The 1 Thing That Some Charities Won't Tell You

Instead of using their own employees to raise money, some charities will hire professional solicitors. Charities that do hire these solicitors direct millions of dollars away annually from worthwhile causes to pay them off.

CHAPTER 9

Make a Full-Time Income Working Part-Time Hours

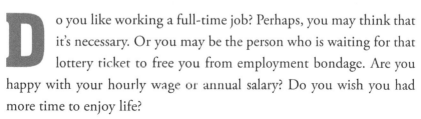

D o you like working a full-time job? Perhaps, you may think that it's necessary. Or you may be the person who is waiting for that lottery ticket to free you from employment bondage. Are you happy with your hourly wage or annual salary? Do you wish you had more time to enjoy life?

Wouldn't it be great to earn a full time income while working part time hours? What could you see yourself doing during that time off? You could go to the beach, hike up a mountain, spend more time volunteering for your favorite charity, or maybe a sunny picnic with your significant other.

What if you could work part time hours and still earn a full time income? The methods that I'm about to provide may not be a good fit for everyone. They will probably work best for college students, the underemployed, the unemployed, and anyone who is currently making less than $50k a year.

The first way that you could achieve this feat is by being a salesperson. Most of sales positions include commission compensation, whether it's with or without a salary. Some sales positions allow you to earn passive income on all of your sales while others only allow you to earn one-time commissions.

One example is The Dump*, a discount furniture chain that has locations in 7 states. Part time salespeople can earn a full time salary working 3 days a week. The Dump's stores are only open 3 days a week, from Friday to Sunday, when customers are likely to shop. They pay their employees a base pay of $10 an hour, which gives job applicants confidence to stay ahead of their bills even if they have a slow weekend. According to E.J. Strelitz (the company's CEO), their top salesperson earns $110,000 annually. While everyone may not be currently capable of earning commissions that will yield them a 6 figure annual salary, salespeople can still do well.

The Dump is just one of many examples. Some people may opt for doing sales for a company like Amway*, Avon*, or Youngevity*. The compensation will vary depending on the company but people who possess the aptitude for sales often do well.

The second way that you could achieve this feat is by being a food demonstrator. A food demonstrator is a person who educates customers about the product and entices them by offering them a sample. Demo companies will pitch their services to various food manufacturers in order to gain clients. These interested companies may want more exposure in grocery stores to expand brand awareness and increase sales. Once an agreement has been reached, the demo company will hire a team to execute the event.

Food demonstrators typically work 3 to 8 hour shifts, 2 to 4 days a week. Food demonstrators either work directly for the food manufacturer or through an independent food demo company. Demonstrators that work directly for the food companies are very likely to make more money than other demonstrators working for third party companies. The hourly wage for these positions can be as low as $11 and as high as $25 an hour.

Most demo companies will start off a new demonstrator with weekend shifts. If they are impressed with the demonstrator's performance, then their hours may gradually increase over time. If there is a flexible cap on the company's marketing budget, the demonstrator may get up to working 4 days a week, doing 6 hour demos. So, if a demonstrator is getting $20 an hour, they will earn $480.00 a week. Keep in mind that working directly for a food manufacturer may grant you other opportunities to make even more money. Some food manufacturers may include bonuses and/or commissions along with their base pay to incentivize demonstrators to give their best performance.

Independent demo companies are likely to offer more demonstrator positions than food manufacturers. There are 3 types of independent demo companies. The first type is national demo companies. These companies are usually based in most states. Sunflower Staffing is one of these companies. Their large presence is attributed to their list of targeted stores, which include Walmart, Ralphs, Target, Kroger, Sam's Club, and Publix. The second type is regional demo companies. These companies are usually based in several states within that region. Natural Selection Promotions is one of these companies and currently covers 14 states. The last type is local demo companies. These companies are usually based only in that state. JP Marketing is one of these companies. They service the state of Texas and conduct demos in the cities of Austin, Houston, San Antonio, Dallas, and Fort Worth.

In some cities, both independent demo companies and food manufacturers may list their job opportunities on Craigslist. The one thing that demonstrators enjoy about these positions is that there is little or no overhead. If you are working directly for a food manufacturer or for an independent demo company, it is very unlikely that you will have an on-site supervisor. You may be trained by the boss or another demonstrator during your first day. However, after that initial training, you are usually on your own. Depending on the company, some demonstrators may be offered advancement opportunities.

Some companies will require you to obtain a food handler's certification prior to working. It's the law in some states and companies must comply to stay in business. Most of these positions are W9, which means you are responsible for paying your own taxes.

Independent food demo companies that hire demonstrators:

- Sunflower Staffing* (national)
- Natural Selection Promotions* (regional—14 Western states)
- JP Marketing* (local: TX)
- Four Star Demos* (local: TX)
- Chuck Latham Associates*
- RC Marketing and Promotions*
- Advantage Sales and Marketing* (national)
- At Your Service Marketing* (regional: TX, OK, LA)
- Campaigners*
- Confero*
- Kit Moss Productions* (regional: IA, IL, IN, MN, ND, SD, WI)
- Muscle Marketing*
- New Concepts in Marketing*
- Quality Marketing Group*

The third way that you can achieve this feat is by being an alcohol demonstrator. This position is very similar to a food demonstrator. Instead of food, you'll be educating customers about a particular alcohol beverage and entice them by offering them a sample. Alcohol demonstrators typically work 3 to 4 hour shifts, 2 to 4 days a week. They either work directly for the company or through an independent alcohol demo company. The hourly wage for these positions can be as low as $15 and up to $30 an hour.

Some companies will require you to obtain an alcohol compliance certification prior to working. It's the law in most areas and companies must comply to stay in business. The TIPS certification is accepted and available in most states except Hawaii, New Mexico, Vermont, and New Hampshire. Most of these positions are W9, which means you are responsible for paying your own taxes.

Independent alcohol demo companies that hire demonstrators:
- Advantage Sales and Marketing* (national)
- BARetc*
- Bon Affair*
- Eurpac Service*
- Interactions*
- Legacy Marketing Partners*
- Ogilvyaction*
- PMG Retail and Entertainment* (local: TX)
- PromoWorks*
- Salespros*
- Spotlite Agency*
- Sweet Revenge*
- Tallgrass Talent Group*

The fourth way that you can achieve this feat is by being a brand ambassador. A brand ambassador is a person who represents a brand for a company at a special event. There are other job titles like promotional models and product demonstrators, which are used interchangeably with the title, brand ambassador. Promotional companies will pitch their services to various companies in order to gain clients. These interested companies may want more exposure in a target area to expand brand awareness. Sometimes, they will specifically wait for annual events because they are likely to get a better return on their investment. Once an agreement has been reached, the promotional company will hire a team to execute the event.

While a few promotional companies may offer constant flow of promotional work, most brand ambassadors will work for multiple promotional companies to get constant flow of work. The majority of brand ambassador positions are through promotional companies but there are few positions that are obtained by going through a company directly. There are multiple Fortune 500 companies that hire brand ambassadors directly. Sometimes, these positions pay more but there is usually more responsibility that is involved too. The hourly wage for these positions can be as low as $14 and as high as $25 an hour.

Some promotional companies are more selective than others. Typically, newer promotional companies are likely to be more lenient in hiring brand ambassadors than their renowned competitors. Some companies will hire the same group of brand ambassadors for their events. This is good for the brand ambassadors because it allows them to strengthen their relationships and build their reputation with the promotional company. Your relationships and reputation is what will determine your success as a brand ambassador.

Brand ambassadors will make the most money when they are hired to do promotional tours. A promotional tour is one event that is conducted in multiple cities. They can make anywhere from $2000 to $5000 per tour. You can make even more if the tour goes beyond 30 days. I have several friends who are college students or recently graduated from college that are doing these tours. I know somebody who graduated from college but chose to do these tours for a living. He graduated with an engineering degree and probably wouldn't have any trouble finding a great career. He simply told me, "I do 10 to 12 tours a year and end up grossing $40,000 a year for working 8 months. I have 4 months off a year and love the freedom that it offers." Please keep in mind that a good reputation as well as good relationships is what will you get to earn that type of salary.

In some cities, promotional companies may list their job opportunities on Craigslist. Some companies have their own online portals that allow you to register as a brand ambassador. Once you're registered, you'll get emails sent to your inbox about upcoming promotional events in your area. While most promotional companies have a website, some of them will only result to an email list as the sole form of recruiting.

The one thing that brand ambassadors enjoy about these positions is the fun work environment. I have done enough of these events to tell you about the types of assignments. For one client, I was passing out coupons and samples for one of the biggest boxed snack companies. The objective was to be friendly to people while giving out coupons and samples. I did that assignment for 2 days for a total of 10 hours and got paid $300. For another client, I did a guerrilla marketing campaign for one of the top cell phone providers. The objective was to canvass 2 universities with a friendly demeanor and pass out leaflets. I did that assignment for 3 days for a total of 12 hours and got paid $500. As you have seen in my prior experiences, these jobs don't require a lot of skill or intelligence. Having a likable personality and a great attitude is usually all that is required from you.

The next level up from a brand ambassador is a team leader, more commonly known as a team lead. For some promotional companies, the team lead also serves as the on-site supervisor. They manage the event and supervise the brand ambassadors. For other promotional companies, the team lead plays a lesser role. This is the case if a tour manager is involved. The team lead in this case will only assure that all brand ambassadors are present and have submitted their timesheets. The team lead usually get paid $1 to $3 more per hour than brand ambassadors.

The next level up from a team lead is a market manager. A market manager is the on-site supervisor for all of the events held in that city. They manage the events and supervise the brand ambassadors. Most market managers are salaried employees. Every promotional company does not have market managers. Team leaders and tour managers sometimes act as market managers.

The next level up from a market manager is a tour manager. Some promotional companies may have 2 tour managers for the tour, one serving as an assistant tour manager and the other serving as the leading tour manager. The tour manager is usually required to have a commercial driver license (also known as a CDL). They are responsible for the setup and the breakdown of each event. Some tours are limited to a region like New England, the Southwest, or the East Coast, while some tours are nationwide. Tour managers can make anywhere from $2800 to $4000 a month, depending on the company and the person's experience.

Most of these promotional events are fun and easy. Some of these positions are W4 (meaning taxes already taken out) or W9 (meaning you will receive the gross amount and are responsible for paying your own taxes). Please note that most recruiters are expecting to get a promotional resume from you. Do not send them your standard resume. If you send them your standard resume, your resume will likely get pushed off to the side. Recruiters do care about your qualifications but they are more interested in the promotional events that you have worked in the past. A good promotional resume will definitely increase your chances of getting hired for the event.

Promotional companies that hire promotional staff:

- EventPro Strategies*
- Productions Plus*
- Attack Marketing*
- Fusion Event Staffing*
- Mosaic*
- Marketing Werks*
- All Aces Promotional Staffing*
- Team Marketing*
- GMR Marketing*
- Adelante Live*
- GC Marketing*
- Push Models*

*I do not endorse any of the companies mentioned. Since I have heard mixed reviews about them, I will recommend that you do your own due diligence before moving forward with any of these companies.

CHAPTER 10

Work From Home For The Rest Of Your Life

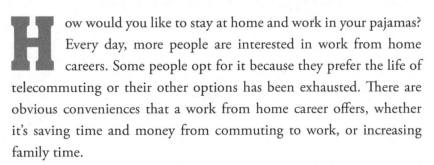

How would you like to stay at home and work in your pajamas? Every day, more people are interested in work from home careers. Some people opt for it because they prefer the life of telecommuting or their other options has been exhausted. There are obvious conveniences that a work from home career offers, whether it's saving time and money from commuting to work, or increasing family time.

Flexibility is a huge benefit to working at home. Most jobs have fixed work hours. Some of the companies that are mentioned in this chapter will allow you to work split shifts to accommodate your schedule.

One of the greatest benefits about working at home is the money that you'll save in expenses.

Food expenses. More than half of people spend at least $5 to buy breakfast and/or lunch during their work shift. When you are working at home, your food expenses will go down since you'll be much more likely to make those meals at home.

Transit expenses. More than half of people use public transit or drive to work every day. When you are working at home, you can save money on fuel, parking and maintenance costs. You also may save money on car insurance if your insurer offers a reduced rate for fewer miles driven each month. Public transit users can save money on fares.

Child care expenses. More than one-third of people pay for some form of child care. When you are working at home, you can save money by keeping your kids occupied with something while you are working.

You might be convinced that working home is right for you. Can you picture yourself sitting at your home desk with your favorite cup of coffee in your most comfortable clothing? Can you see yourself having your breaks on your porch or in your living room? You don't have to worry about office politics because you'll never be at the office! When your workday is over, you can go about doing what you normally would without worrying about commuting. This is how I live everyday and you can too!

There are 2 ways to get started. The first way to start is by a slow transition. You can take a part-time work from home job as secondary income. You can try it to see if you like it. If so, transitioning into full-time work shouldn't be difficult at all. The second way is go straight for a full-time work from home position. This is probably best for people who are currently unemployed or need to stay at home to care for their children.

As with any job, there are always expectations, even for virtual positions. Most of these companies require that you work in a quiet environment. This is especially true for call center positions. They expect you to be a self-starter and a problem solver who requires little to no supervision. Are you good at managing your own time? You will be expected to have good time management skills. Sometimes, it can be easy to fall into distractions that will take you away from work. It will be your job to police yourself.

If you can be a good steward of time, working virtually can be quite enjoyable. You may decide to spend a weekend in Houston and get some non-phone work done. You may choose to go to the beach and get some administrative work done by the water. Working virtually can give you work environment diversity.

A lot of work at home employers don't differ from brick and mortar employers. They offer the same great benefits like paid vacation time, medical coverage, and even tuition assistance programs with some employers. There are some of these employers who may only hire independent contractors, which will make you ineligible for the benefits that were previously mentioned.

Some companies may require a small monetary investment in order to get started. You should never pay any money to the company for work. However, there are some equipment supplies that are needed if you are going to be doing call center work. Most employers may require you to have a headset, high speed internet connection, and a dedicated phone line. Some employers want you to have a computer system that meets certain requirements. Any equipment supplies bought for at-home work can also be used as a tax write-off. There are several companies that require a background and/or credit check. They may provide a link for you to purchase this report and request that it be sent to them.

It is important to realize that some employers will only hire during certain seasons. A lot of at-home workers work for more than 1 company to assure a constant flow of income. While there are some employers that offer full-time positions, it's important to take several part-time jobs if you're unable to secure a full-time position.

The most common work from home positions is call center representatives. Eddie Bauer, Comcast, and the Home Shopping Network (HSN) are some of the companies that use West at Home to handle customer service and online ordering. West at Home has been known to be a good company for entry level employees. If you have a special skill set that involves any form of medical training, you may have a good chance in securing a work from home position with a health organization or health insurance company.

As stated before, some companies have hiring seasons and only hire during that time. So, even if you felt that you did everything right, the employer may not get back to you immediately. Many of these employers accept online applications every day, which they keep handy when they're ready to hire again.

In this next section, I will share the types of at-home work, the companies that hire these types, their requirements and benefits.

Call Center Representatives

Most call center companies typically offer work opportunities that involves inbound call work. This is where you would receive phone calls on your home phone with a headset and use your computer to process any orders and answer any customer service related questions. There are a few companies that offer both inbound and outbound call work. With outbound call work, employers may give preference to applicants with cold calling and sales experience.

The basic requirements for this type of work is to have a quiet office space, a computer system that meets company's specifications, a headset with a microphone, and the ability to type at least 35 words per minute.

Employers

1800 Flowers offers full-time and part-time work at home opportunities in 12 states. However, the majority of their available positions are seasonal. You must be at least 18 years old with a high school diploma or equivalent to apply. They offer paid training as well as sales commissions on the top of an employee's base pay, which is $9 an hour. (Employees who are bilingual are usually paid more). Based on employees' reviews, About.com gives 1800 Flowers 3.25 out of 5 stars.

Accolade hires part-time independent contractors in the U.S. only. A voice audition is required to determine that you have their desired professional voice tone. They offer paid training and a starting pay of $7.25 to $9 an hour. Based on employees' reviews, Glassdoor gives Accolade 3.2 out of 5 stars.

ACD Direct hires call center reps to take pledges for companies like NPR, PBS, and Saint Jude Children's Hospital. You are paid by the actual minute of phone time, usually 25 to 32 cents a minute. So, downtime between calls is not paid. Based on employees' reviews, Glassdoor gives ACD Direct 3.3 out of 5 stars.

Alpine Access hires customer service reps for inbound calls only in the United States and Canada. The company hires their representatives as full-time employees with an extensive benefit package. New employees are required to do 3-6 weeks of paid training. The position pays $9 an hour and payments are made biweekly.

Amazon recruits call center reps and call center managers. They hire both permanent and temporary employees. Call center reps are entry level positions while call center managers require a bachelor's degree and 2 years of related experience to be considered. To be considered for one of their positions, you must live in one of the following states: Arizona, Delaware, Kansas, Kentucky, New York, North Dakota, Oregon, Washington, or West Virginia.

American Express hires customer care professionals to work from home in the District of Columbia and the continental U.S. (excluding California). Employees can earn an average of $16.13 per hour or more based on their prior work experience and job performance with

American Express. They enjoy a generous benefit package, retirement programs, along with comprehensive medical, dental, and vision plans. This is probably the best call center position available.

Apple hires full-time and part-time at-home advisors in a virtual call center. At-Home Advisors assess issues and troubleshoot them. They provide support for iPhone, iPod, iPad, iMac, MacBook Pro, Mac Pro, AirPort, and Apple TV. Bilingual skills can be a plus in getting one of these positions. Some of their desired languages are French, German, Japanese, Portuguese, and Spanish. Apple provides an iMac for use while working from home. They offer a generous benefits package and employee discounts on Apple products.

Below are some of Apple's recruiting metro areas:
- Birmingham, Hoover, and Troy (*AL*)
- Tempe and Tucson (*AZ*)
- Benton and Little Rock (*AR*)
- Sacramento and San Diego (*CA*)
- Colorado Springs (*CO*)
- Fort Lauderdale, Fort Myers, Gainesville, Miami, and Orlando (*FL*)
- Atlanta, Augusta, Kennesaw, and Marietta (*GA*)
- Honolulu (*HI*)
- Chicago and Champaign (*IL*)
- Fort Wayne and Lafayette (*IN*)
- Des Moines (*IA*)
- Wichita (*KS*)
- Louisville (*KY*)
- Baton Rouge (*LA*)
- Springfield (*MA*)
- Detroit and Grand Rapids (*MI*)
- Kansas City (*MO*)

- Asheville (*NC*)
- Grand Forks (*ND*)
- Omaha (*NE*)
- Albuquerque (*NM*)
- Las Vegas (*NV*)
- Albany (*NY*)
- Oklahoma City and Tulsa (*OK*)
- Cleveland, Columbus, and Toledo (*OH*)
- Eugene and Portland (*OR*)
- Allentown and Philadelphia (*PA*)
- Providence (*RI*)
- Charlestown and Summerville (*SC*)
- Knoxville, Memphis, and Nashville (*TN*)
- Austin, Dallas, Houston, McAllen, and San Antonio (*TX*)
- Salt Lake City (*UT*)
- Seattle and Spokane (*WA*)
- Milwaukee (*WI*)
- Casper (*WY*)

Some of the college campuses where Apple recruits include:
- University of Arizona
- Arizona State University
- California State University
- San Diego State University
- Louisiana State University
- Texas State University
- Texas A&M University
- University of Florida, Gainesville
- University of Georgia, Athens
- University of Oregon, Eugene
- University of Nevada, Las Vegas

- University of New Mexico
- University of Utah

Arise is a hub for hundreds of independent businesses. Those independent businesses that partner with Arise hires client support professionals for customer service. Wages and benefits will vary depending on the independent business. You can go to Arise's official website to learn more about their partners.

ARO hires full-time and part-time call center reps. They offer paid training that lasts 6-10 weeks long. The pay rate for training will be the same when you're finished with the training ($9-$10 an hr).

Aspire Lifestyles hires only employees from the following states: AL, AZ, CO, DE, FL, GA, IL, IN, KY, MA, MI, MO, NC, NH, OH, OR, PA, SC, TN, TX, UT, VA, WA, WI. They pay $8.50 an hour plus commission. They only offer part-time hours (up to 34 hours a week) and require that you work weekends and some holidays. They offer paid training at the state or federal minimum wage, whichever is higher.

Blue Zebra hires independent contractors that have 2 years of B2B sales and cold calling experience. They pay $15-$25 an hour based upon experience and skill level. They pay weekly and offer direct deposit.

Brighten Communications hires independent contractors that are comfortable doing B2B sales. Their typical work hours are 8am to 5pm, Monday to Friday. They pay weekly at an hourly rate of $12-$16 an hour.

Cloud 10 hires employees to take customer service calls. Employees are paid biweekly at an hourly rate of $9-$12 an hour, working 32-38 hours per week on a set schedule. Priority consideration is given to applicants that speak another language fluently.

Convergys hires full-time and part-time employees as call center reps. U.S. reps are paid weekly at $9 an hour. There are opportunities to advance within the company. They offer many benefits to their employees, including medical, dental, vision, basic life insurance, short and long term disability insurance, tuition reimbursement, 401k, and an employee stock purchase plan.

Kelly at Home offers full-time and part-time opportunities. They offer many benefits to their employees, including medical, prescription, group life insurance, referral bonuses, Kudos! (their employee reward program), employee discounts, and paid time off (vacation, holiday, and sick pay).

LiveOps hires call center reps as independent contractors. Their typical pay rate is $0.25 per minute, which means that downtime between calls are not paid. They do offer you the opportunity to earn more money based on your ability to upsell during calls. They pay biweekly by check or direct deposit.

NCO Group hires call center reps as employees. Their benefit package is available to their employees after 90 days of employment. Full-time employees are automatically enrolled in the company's paid benefits of group life, accidental death and dismemberment, and long term disability insurance. NCO offer employees the option to enroll in their other benefits, such as pre-tax medical, dental, vision, and short term disability insurance. Benefits provided to employees will also cover their spouse and children. The pay rate for these positions is not disclosed by the company nor were we able to hear from former employees regarding their experiences.

NEW Corp hires full-time and part-time reps as employees. They pay $9.50 an hour. They provide 6 weeks of paid training, which is also paid at your starting hourly rate. You can work as little as 20 hours or up to 40 hours a week. If hired, you will be required to work evenings and weekends.

Pearl Interactive Network hires full-time and part-time call center reps for B2B sales. They are known to give preference to disabled veterans and military wives. Prior call center experience is not required.

Their work week is Monday to Friday. The pay rate for these positions is not disclosed by the company nor were we able to hear from former employees regarding their experiences.

Sitel hires full-time and part-time call center reps as employees. At-home employees take inbound customer service calls by providing billing service, account inquiries, and product orders or inquiries. The company gives preference to applicants that are fluent in French, German, Italian, Korean, Mandarin, Portuguese, or Spanish. Sitel expects all reps to work a 5 day work week (including one weekend day). The benefits for full-time employees include a 401k, vacation/holiday pay, medical/dental, and employee discounts. Sitel pays their call center reps an hourly wage of $9-$10 an hour and hire in all states except AK, CA, HI, MA, MT, NH, ND, OH, OR, RI, VT, WV, and WY.

Teleflora hires call center reps to meet seasonal demands. While they pay their call center reps $8-$11 an hour, they offer paid training at the state's minimum wage of the new employee. Teleflora hires a lot of temporary staff especially before Mother's Day, Easter, Christmas, and Valentine's Day. However, they do have at-home employees that work year round.

TeleNetwork hires full-time and part-time reps in Arizona, Colorado, Florida, Kansas, Texas, Utah, and the Carolinas. While the company will hire applicants with no prior experience, they tend to give priority to applicants with prior experience. The company pays $8-$9 an hour with the opportunity to earn commission on upsells. They pay biweekly via direct deposit. After 6 months of employment, employees will acquire benefits including healthcare, vacation/holiday pay, and a 401k plan.

TeleTech hires call centers reps as employees for sales, customer service, and technical support. The company gives preference to applicants that are bilingual. They pay $9-$10 an hour with online paid training provided. The company requires employees to work at least 20 hours and on some weekends or holidays. TeleTech hires in all states except AK, CA, DE, HI, IA, IN, MA, ME, NH, NJ, OR, RI, and VT.

U-Haul hires part-time call center reps to assist customers with moving questions and scheduling. They prefer people who can work at least 25 hours a week including some weekends. Their pay rate varies from $7.50 to $15 an hour, with the higher pay including sales bonuses. They offer paid training which lasts 4 weeks and gives employees a $50 bonus upon completion. After 3 months of employment, you get a certain benefit package depending on your full-time or part-time status.

West at Home hires part-time call center reps as employees. They pay their reps between $0.12 to $0.30 cents a minute and hire in 25 states (AL, AZ, AR, CO, FL, GA, IA, IN, KS, KY, LA, MD, ME, MI, MO, MS, NC, NE, NJ, OK, SC, TN, TX, UT, VA). Keep in mind that they do not hire in all counties in these states. Please visit their website for more information regarding their hiring counties within those states.

Working Solutions hires call center reps as independent contractors for sales, customer service, and technical support. The company gives preference to applicants that are bilingual. Their pay rate ranges from $7.50 to $30 an hour, depending on the project. While employees can choose their hours online, the availability of hours can vary which may make it difficult in earning a full-time income. They pay biweekly by check or direct deposit.

Google Raters

Google Raters don't typically work for Google but for a third party company that rates search results that come up in the search engine. Then, Google uses that provided information to improve search engine results. The pay rate is usually $12-$16 an hour with the stipulation that the hourly requirement for pages rated is met. While this job can have different type of tasks, the basic tasks are typing keywords in Google and evaluating the quality of the pages that come up.

The basic requirement for this type of work is to have a high speed internet connection. Some of the companies that hire Google raters may have their own hardware requirements.

Employers

Appen Butler Hill hires part-time Google raters as independent contractors. They must be an U.S. native and work at least 20 hours a week but the scheduling of those hours is quite flexible. According to Glassdoor, it appears that the hourly rate for this position is $13-$15 an hour. They pay once a month via check or direct deposit.

Leapforce hires part-time Google raters as independent contractors. In order to remain working at Leapforce, raters must remain active by completing a minimum of 200 evaluation tasks every 30 days. According to Glassdoor, it appears that the hourly rate for this position is $13-$14 an hour. They pay once a month via check.

Lionbridge hires part-time Google raters as independent contractors. Applicants must speak fluent English, have high speed internet, work 10-20 hours per week, and be a resident of your country for at least 5 consecutive years. They offer training but it is unpaid. According to previous employees' experience, the pay rate is $13-$14 an hour. They pay once a month via bank wire transfer. (Keep in mind that you are likely to incur charges when receiving a wire transfer).

ZeroChaos hires part-time Google raters as employees. Each new hire is given a 1 year contract, along with a 3 month intermission. After the intermission, the rater can reapply to work for the company again. ZeroChaos pays raters $15 an hour and requires them to work 10-30 hours a week. They pay biweekly by direct deposit or Paypal.

Transcriptionists

In today's society, we are fortunate to have access to transcription software but there still lies a need for experienced online transcriptionists to overcome non-human errors. The finance, legal, and medical industries are just a few fields that still require transcribers. Most companies will hire transcriptionists as independent contractors. One of the advantages in working as a transcriptionist is that many companies will allow you to set your own schedule. However, one of the greatest disadvantages is that you may need prior transcription experience and/or prior experience in the medical or legal industries to be hired.

Some companies might require a certain type of computer or software package, proficiency in a certain software program, and a transcription foot pedal, which can cost you about $75.

Employers

Accutran Global hires transcriptionists as independent contractors. It is an entry level position with a 70 wpm typing requirement. The company recommends transcriptionists to use a transcription foot pedal. Training is paid but it is withheld for 6 months. Transcriptionists will be paid $50 for their training after earning $2,000 in the first 6 months. Work is available in 2 shifts: the AM shift (4a-2p) and the PM shift (4:30p-7:30p). More work is available throughout the day during peak season. The pay rate for transcriptionists is $0.005-$0.006 per word and paid on a calendar month basis on the 15th of the following month by check or Paypal.

Birch Creek Communications hires transcriptionists as independent contractors. One of the major perks of this company is their flexibility. Transcriptionists can accept jobs according to their availability. The rates of pay vary depending on the job, turnaround time, and the quality of your work. For corporate and financial clients, the company pays by the audio minute, ranging from $0.40-$1.25 per minute. For legal clients, the company pays by the page, ranging from $0.75-$1.75 per page.

Cambridge Transcriptionists hires part-time transcriptionists that have legal and corporate experience. Legal transcriptionists are required to have at least 1 year of legal transcription or court reporting experience. Prior experience is not necessary for corporate transcriptionists. However, the company will give priority to applicants with experience in transcribing legal, medical, or technical documents.

Fast Chart hires medical transcriptionists as independent contractors. The company requires applicants to have at least 2 years of full-time medical transcription experience in a hospital or clinical setting. Some of the company's benefits are shift differential pay, premium holiday and weekend pay, and incentive pay. Fast Chart pays biweekly via direct deposit.

Quicktate hires transcriptionists as independent contractors. The company will not consider any applicant that has a misdemeanor or felony on their record. Quicktate hires new and experienced transcriptionists. They pay $0.025-$0.050 per word. Once you've become seasoned at Quicktate, you can move onto iDictate, who hires experienced transcriptionists at $0.050 per word.

Scribie hires transcriptionists as independent contractors. They hire new and experienced transcriptionists. They pay $10 per audio hour of transcription and a monthly bonus of $10 for every 3 hours completed. You can be promoted to a reviewer after 1 audio hour of raw transcript submissions with an average grade of 3.25. Scribie pays transcriptionists within 1 business day via Paypal.

SpeakWrite hires general and legal transcriptionists as independent contractors. The company offers enough work to do it on a full-time basis. The pay rate is $0.050 per word, which turns out to be $12-$15 an hour depending on your speed and ability. With experience and improvement, transcriptionists can go on to make $15+ an hour. SpeakWrite pays twice a month via check or direct deposit.

Teachers / Tutors

Every year, online teaching has been increasing in demand. It is probably the most convenient way for people to access education or tutoring. Parents hire tutors because they usually don't have time to tutor their children. Most adult students have busy work schedules and always looking for cheaper and convenient ways to educate themselves. Virtual teachers and tutors meet all of these needs and offer their services through distance learning institutions.

You can earn a good supplemental income as a teacher or tutor if you are relentless about it. Teaching qualifications will vary due to company's requirements for applicants. Some institutions will require that you have a college degree and/or prior teaching experience. Other institutions will allow you to use your special skill set to create your own course and teach it for compensation.

Teachers/tutors and students meet online via instant messenger or VOIP chat (i.e. Skype). The teaching and tutoring opportunities are numerous. You can help high school students prepare for SAT/ACT exams, teach or tutor students at the collegiate level, or teach continuing education courses. It is likely that you will be limited to part-time hours unless you are a degreed professional hired to work at a higher education institution or have a consistent stream of multiple teaching/tutoring gigs.

Employers

Argosy University hires online adjunct professors for psychology, business, education, health sciences, and criminal justice courses. Candidates must have previous teaching experience and possess a master's degree for undergraduate programs and a doctorate degree for graduate programs. For specialty courses, industry experience is preferred. They do not accept applications from applicants residing in Iowa, Kentucky, and North Carolina.

Capella University hires online dissertation mentors and adjunct professors. They offer great employee benefits, which includes the minimum of 17 paid days off, paid parental leave, choice of medical and dental plans, short and long-term disability insurance, 401k retirement plan, tuition reimbursement for Capella courses, and employee reward programs.

Course Bridge hires instructors as independent contractors to provide their own courses to the website. Instructors can create courses on topics of their choice as well as keep all of their intellectual property rights. They are paid 70% of the base registration fee per student for the course and 55% of registrations processed through partner and affiliate sites. Instructors are paid once a month by check or Paypal.

Go Fluent hires online business English trainers. Applicants who are bilingual are given priority consideration. Their most desired languages are French, Japanese, Korean, Portuguese and Russian. They are currently hiring in most areas of the following states: Florida, Kansas, Missouri, Oregon, New York, and Washington. Applicants must be willing to work a minimum of 20 hours a week.

Instructional Connections hires part-time online academic coaches as independent contractors. Applicant's requirements will vary depending on the prospective position. The position acts in a much similar fashion to that of a teaching assistant, serving as the student's initial point of contact. Academic coaches who consistently complete assignment with quality will be considered for promotion to a lead coach or coordinating coach, which will entail more sections and/or responsibilities.

ITT Tech hires online adjunct professors. They require applicants to have at least master's degree to be considered for most of their available positions. They offer great employee benefits, which include health insurance (medical, dental, vision, prescriptions), short and long-term disability insurance, health savings account, life insurance, 401k, paid time off, and tuition reimbursement and discounts.

Kaplan University hires online adjunct professors. They require applicants to have at least master's degree to be considered for most of their available positions. They offer some of the best employee benefits, which include health insurance (medical, dental, vision), life insurance, short and long-term disability insurance, paid time off (including holidays, vacation, sick and personal days, bereavement and jury duty leave), 401k, long-term care insurance, free Kaplan courses, employee discounts, and paid bonuses for employee referrals.

Southern New Hampshire University hires online adjunct professors. Teaching assignments may be temporary, part-time, and/ or on-call and may be immediate or as needed. Adjunct professors are paid $2,200 per 9 week undergraduate course and $2,500 per 10 week graduate course. Nursing courses has a separate compensation structure. Professors are considered W2 employees and are paid biweekly.

South University hires online adjunct professors. Applicants must have prior teaching experience and at least a master's degree including 18 graduate credits in the area of the applicant's intended teaching subject. For specialty courses, industry experience is preferred.

Universal Class hires content creators as independent contractors. This is slightly different but still relevant since you're still providing educational content to students. They post projects on their website and wait for people to bid on them. If they accept the bid, the winning bidder is expected to produce the project within 60 days. Upon verification of the delivered product, the winning bidder is paid via Paypal or check. Most of their projects pay thousands of dollars.

University of California-Berkeley Extension hires online instructors for their international diploma programs. They require applicants to have a graduate degree, teaching experience, and professional experience in their field. Some of the employee's benefits at

UC Berkeley are free admission and discounts to UC museums, athletic and cultural events.

Writers

A lot of people enjoy writing but typically never get paid for it. Some people enjoy it as a hobby and others grow fond of it during their years in school. This is an area that I think passion plays an important role. You surely can just do it for the money but you're not likely to find it enjoyable.

It is important for any aspiring writer to have good grammar skills. If you are a good writer, content writing can eventually become a full-time income for you. Most of the online writing that new writers will do is website content optimized for search engines. Businesses and website owners will pay you to write 250-500 word articles to get ranked in higher Google search results. Since there are many companies that pay writers for content, you can find a company that will allow you to write about a topic of your choice. However, if you are not an expert in a particular field, it shouldn't take more than 10 minutes to write an informative article about an unfamiliar subject.

There are 2 types of compensation structures for freelance writers: upfront pay and residual pay. *Upfront pay* is a one-time payment to the original author, who will give away exclusive rights to the buyer of the content. When there is an ongoing relationship between the original author and the client, the original author is commonly known as the ghostwriter. *Residual pay* is typically monthly payments made to the author for the amount of page views generated by the author's content.

What if you really want to be a writer but have no experience? Fear not. Many companies will test your skills and start you off on an appropriate level. During that time, you will have the opportunity to develop your skills to see if writing is a realistic career for you. Please keep in mind that your skill level is pegged to your pay level. This is why

I stated earlier that passion play an important role as a writer, especially if you're average at best.

Once you have developed your writing skills and have a writing portfolio available, you can qualify for writing projects offered on the following .com sites: Guru, Odesk, and Elance. The projects offered on these sites will vary. Some examples of these writing projects are ghostwriting a print or e-book, creating content directly for a business or individual's website, or writing speeches. If you are a seasoned writer, the 3 websites that I just mentioned may be all that you need to earn a full-time income.

If you are not a seasoned writer, it would be a good idea to start with the employers listed in this chapter to develop a writing portfolio. Then, you can use that experience as a launching pad to qualify for the advanced writing projects.

Employers

About.com is looking for experienced online writers who are credible authorities in their field. If you are hired, you will likely start off at the lowest level as a topic guide.

Topic guides write content on specialized topics. All topic guides are expected to write 6 to 10 articles a month and expected to promote their content. In their first 2 years, topic guides are paid by the article. After that period, they are likely to receive compensation for page views above and beyond the minimum pay per article. The next level up from this position is the guide.

Guides have the same responsibilities of a topic guide, in addition to creating a weekly newsletter and moderating a discussion forum on a particular topic. They get a guaranteed per article rate (not including performance incentives). The new guide can expect to earn about $1000 a month during their first 2 years. The average guide can expect about

$2000 a month while the top guides earn $4000+ a month. The next level up from this position is the video producer.

Video producers produce premium video content that is 1 to 3 minutes. They are paid a flat fee of $250 per accepted HD video. About.com recommends that producers use Adobe Photoshop for image editing and Final Cut Pro for video post-production.

About.com guides are paid on a monthly basis while video producers are paid on the 15th and 30th of every month.

ClickNWork hires experienced writers. The company often has a need for a wide range of writers that specializes in a certain industry like business (in food, sustainability, or consumerism), health and wellness, and innovation. They have 2 streams of work, *planned* and *ad hoc*. Most of the work received from clients is *planned*, which means it's reliable since it's a set number of hours weekly or monthly. The rest of the work received is considered *ad hoc*, which means it's erratic and often used to fulfill time-sensitive client assignments. The pay depends on a consultant's experience and the assignment complexity, which can range from $4-$40 an hour. They pay via Paypal or bank account once a month.

Demand Studios hires experienced writers to provide content for websites like LIVESTRONG.com and eHow. Writers are provided with opportunities for growth. Other than your writing experience, the only other requirement for writers is to have professional experience, writing experience, or an education (in the form of a degree or certification) in one of their 20+ categories. Writers usually get paid anywhere from $15 to $20 per article. They get paid twice a week via Paypal.

Geis Writers hires writers with an industry background to write practice test questions for exams. Writers are paid by performance and not hourly.

HubPages is always looking for writers to contribute great content to their site. They have a publishing platform that allows writers to create pages (also known as hubs) on topics of their interest.

Writers earn 60% of the revenue of the pay per views generated from their hubs. They also earn revenue by joining Google's Adsense, HubPages' Ebay and Amazon programs, and from personal referrals. Writers are paid through Paypal once they have reached a minimum payout of $50. Earnings are paid on the 28th of the month following the one in which the payout threshold was achieved. For example, if you reach the minimum in December, you'd be paid that money at the end of January.

The average writer makes about $300 per month. Although, there are writers who make about $2000 per month. As a beginner, I think aiming for making a $100 in your first month is quite realistic in my opinion.

Knoji hires writers as Q&A ambassadors and/or consumer guides.

As a Q&A ambassador, you get paid for participating in their forum discussions. The amount of money that you can earn is based on your seniority (number of your answers and votes received) and the assessment of the quality of your contributions by a Knoji editor. They paid $0.50-$1 for asking questions and up to $1.50 for questions answered.

As a consumer guide, you get paid for creating articles about the quality of products and services from various companies. They pay $0.08-$0.30 cents a word, which turns out to be $50-$200 per article. As you become more of a seasoned writer, you will eventually be able to earn activity bonuses. You can gauge your progress by your current Knoji status. Everyone starts out as a "contributor" and can move up to achieve the highest level of "featured writer", if one is persistent.

Knoji pays monthly via Paypal. There is no minimum amount that you have to earn to get paid for that month.

Skyword hires writers to create content for various brands like Lowe's, Angie's List, Purina, and IBM. The type of pay depends on the brand. Some brands only pay by page views and other brands pay you a flat rate (which is anywhere from $5 to $40 per article). Then, there are brands that pay you a flat rate plus pay by page views. Skyword pays twice monthly via Paypal.

Textbroker hires new and experienced writers. Writers are able to choose their topic of choice based on seniority. Every writer is given a quality level from 1 to 5 stars. You can get paid 0.7 cents a word as a 2 star writer, up to 5 cents a word as a 5 star writer. Your writing sample will determine your initial rating. There are 3 different ways that a writer can earn money: open order, direct order, and team order.

Open order allows you to choose from thousands of orders based on your quality level. This option is best for authors who like a flexible work schedule and want to choose as few or as many projects that are feasible for them.

Direct order allows you to set your own rate per word regardless of your quality level. This option is best for authors who prefer to work with specific clients exclusively and like to receive orders on a regular basis.

Team order allows any author on a team to accept projects on a first come, first serve basis. An author can join as many teams as they wish. The client sets the rate per word for the team. This option is best for authors who regularly want to write for specific clients and/or projects.

Textbroker pays once a week via Paypal, as long as your balance is greater than $10.

The Content Authority hires writers to write articles for various clients. These articles are often posted on blogs and used for print material. The number of available articles to the author is based on their activity and the demand of the client(s). The Content Authority has very basic requirements that will likely qualify most writers. They offer tutorials to help you become a successful writer at their company.

There is no limit on the articles that you can write beyond the limits placed on writers who are on probation. New writers are rated Tier 1, the lowest and probationary level. During this time, you will be limited to Tier 1 type articles. At the end of your probation, your activity and written articles will be reviewed for quality and client feedback. If your writing and feedback indicates a higher tier ranking, you will be promoted (subject to editor discretion).

Writers are paid at a rate according to their tier. However, a Tier 3 writer will not be paid at their tier rate for writing a Tier 1 article. All writers who meet a $25 minimum payout will receive payment every Monday. All writers are considered as independent contractors.

WriterAccess has a business model that is somewhat similar to the company, *Textbroker*. Writers who are accepted receive an initial star rating of 2, 3, 4 or 5, which is determined by the strength of their profiles, writing samples, and initial application and test score. A writer's level can improve (or decline) as assignments are completed.

Writers are paid on a per-word basis for most projects. The client assigns the order a level and writers are paid accordingly. Orders pay anywhere from 1.13 cents up to 4.60 cents per word, depending on the order level. For special projects, clients will normally adjust the compensation to be higher than the standard pay rates. These special projects typically require additional research, industry expertise, or other editorial complexities.

Writers are paid twice a month via Paypal, as long as the balance is at least $10.

Yahoo Voices hires writers as contributors to discuss a variety of topic from your perspective. They will pay you a flat rate if they feel that the content has high marketing potential. The rate is based on search engine optimization (SEO) and reader interest but it is typically $2-$25 (although some partner opportunities may pay up to $100) per article. Writers also can receive residual income on their articles. Yahoo pays $1.50 per thousand page views on Yahoo Voices (where most of your content will be published) and $1.25 per thousand page views on their Yahoo News site. The pay per view rate increases as you become more successful and garner more page views.

Yahoo offers an academy for writers for remedial and enrichment purposes. The academy teaches how to use words for search engine optimization and create attractive content that will keep readers engaged.

Upfront payments are sent daily, Monday-Friday (excluding holidays). If a payment is confirmed too late to be included with a particular day's payments, it will be sent on the following business day. Performance Payments are processed monthly, typically on the second Wednesday of each month, to accounts that have an aggregate performance payment balance of at least $1.50 at the end of the previous month. So, if you had $1.50 accumulated by the last day in April, you would receive that balance on the second Wednesday in May.

Staffing Agencies

A lot of writers may find staffing agencies as the best bang for their buck. Staffing agencies has always been a free service to prospective workers. They work on the behalf of their clients to find skilled writers for various projects. Many employers offer temporary work that may last a few days to a few months. So, it is more cost effective for them to hire a staffing agency rather than hiring part-time or full-time staff. The advantages of working for a staffing agency is getting paid above market rates, doing work for reputable and financially stable employers, having job leads be sent to you, and timely payments.

Filter offers contract and temporary work for freelance copywriters, communications writers, copy editors, and tech writers. The company continually feeds job assignments to their freelancers that match their skills and availability. Interestingly, Filter offer benefits to freelancers like a 401k and health insurance, something that companies typically offer to full-time employees. Based on employees' reviews, Glassdoor gives this company 3.7 out of 5 stars.

The Creative Group offers freelance employment to copywriters. Copywriters work various projects like writing ads and/or web content for pharmaceutical companies, writing product descriptions and/or how-to manuals for big retailers, writing content for direct mail campaigns for media companies, and writing banner ads for online retailers. Based on employees' reviews, Glassdoor gives this company 3 out of 5 stars.

True Talent Group offers freelance employment to copywriters. Copywriters work various projects like writing articles (about finance, wealth management, risk management, and 401ks), magazine ads, teaching aid materials, and direct mail campaigns. This staffing agency typically gives preference to freelancers who live in the local area.

Writing Assistance Inc offers freelance employment to copywriters, medical writers, editors, and technical writers. Based on a writer's skill set, the company will match them with projects offered by regional and national businesses.

Bookkeepers / Accountants / Tax Preparers

Employers

AccountingDepartment.com hires bookkeepers, CPAs, and salespersons as employees. Their work week is Monday to Friday from 8am to 5pm. Employees receive holiday pay after 30 days of service. Paid time off (vacation/sick/personal) is accrued per hour and can be used after 6 months. The company offers a matching 401k plan when the employee has reached their 1 year of service. They do not currently offer medical benefits but it appears that it is something that they will offer soon. Based on employees' reviews, Indeed gives this company 4 out of 5 stars.

Balance Your Books hires bookkeepers, CPAs, and salespersons. Bookkeepers and CPA must have with some prior experience in their industry and using certain software. Salespersons only need have experience with certain software. They offer a competitive salary and a family friendly environment.

Book Minders hires accountants with 4 year degrees and at least 5 years of accounting experience. These positions are limited to applicants who live in the Pittsburgh and Philadelphia metropolitan areas.

Intuit hires tax advisor specialists as employees. They offer some of the best benefits for a company in my opinion. Full-time employees are eligible for all of the mentioned benefits below, while part-time employees are only eligible for certain ones. (If you are considering a part-time position with Intuit, please contact them directly to learn about their benefits for part-time employees).

- Paid time off (holiday and vacation pay, sick leave)
- Free confidential counseling (for personal and work related problems)
- Stock purchase plan (purchase company stock at 15% discount)
- Matching 401k plan (up to $10,000)
- Healthcare coverage (medical, dental, vision, disability, and life insurance)
- Incentive pay (commissions and bonuses on top of one's base salary)
- Loyalty program (service awards in the form of cash and other gifts)
- Parental leave (up to 2 weeks of paid parental leave to care for a newborn or newly adopted child)
- Adoption assistance (up to $3500 reimbursement per adoption)

- Volunteer time off (4 days a year to volunteer in your community)
- Donation matching (up to $2000 a year to most 501c3 non-profits)
- Fitness incentive ($650 per year to offset costs of a gym membership or fitness class fees)
- Tuition assistance (up to $5000 reimbursement per year for career related courses)
- Product discounts (substantial discounts on Intuit and selected software products from Intuit vendors)

Based on employees' reviews, Indeed gives this company 4 out of 5 stars while Glassdoor gives this company 3.7 out of 5 stars. Fortune Magazine ranked Intuit as one of the best employers in 2014.

Administrative Assistants

Online administrative assistants are not very different from virtual assistants. *Administrative assistants* are people who provide administrative support to individuals or businesses. Some of these administrative duties include managing files, sending faxes, preparing business correspondence, and coordinating between departments regarding day-to-day operations. *Virtual assistants* are self-employed individuals who provide administrative assistance to clients from their home office. Some of their responsibilities include file management, data entry, managing correspondence, and coordinating with their boss regarding certain day-to-day operations. Again, these positions are so similar that often these names are used interchangeably.

Employers

Virtual Office Temps hires virtual assistants for their clients and for their own company. They offer a free certification program to applicants in order to get certified and get priority consideration for open positions. Many of these open positions pay $12-$18 per hour. They recommend that virtual assistants to have a professional website regarding their services, since it's typically an industry expectation.

Medical Coders

Medical coders are people who assign certain alphanumeric codes to specific diseases, injuries, and other medical procedures. These assigned codes are often used by international organizations to track the pattern of certain diseases and healthcare costs. Insurance companies rely on these codes to know how much money to reimburse to healthcare providers.

While coding experience wasn't always preferred, it has become a requirement but that's only one of the requirements. A college degree in a health related field may sometimes be required but a certification is a requirement. The professional organization that certifies medical coders are the American Health Information Management Association (AHIMA) and the American Academy of Professional Coders (AAPC).

If a person is determined and has lots of patience, that person can be eligible to be considered for a coder position. Having the aptitude to solve problems effortlessly is important since you will be presented with problems on a daily basis. One of the most important requirements for any medical coder is good "attention to detail" skills. Being very careful about translating medical language to code is crucial because any errors will be of great inconvenience to medical staff, which will cause delayed payments to healthcare providers.

Companies that hire medical coders typically pay at least $10 an hour. However, if you have a relevant educational background and/or prior work experience, you can make anywhere from $12 to $20 an hour. Keep in mind that you will end up with more money when you factor in the savings from working at home.

Employers

Amphion hires full-time and part-time coders. They require that applicants have at least 3 years of recent multi-specialty coding experience. Amphion offers good benefits, which include paid training, 401k, referral bonuses, healthcare (medical, dental, and vision), and tuition reimbursement.

Accentus hires experienced medical coders. They require applicants to have at least 3 years of experience and a coding certification. Based on employees' reviews, Indeed gives this company 4.2 out of 5 stars.

Aviacode hires medical coders as independent contractors. They require applicants to have at least 3 years of experience and at least one certification from the AAPC or the AHIMA. The company pays coders from $18 to $30 an hour. They allow coders to choose their own schedule (whether it's an AM or PM shift or a traditional 8-5 shift). Most of their salaried coding managers and quality assurance supervisors started as medical coders with Aviacode.

Lexicode hires medical coders as employees. The company occasionally provides in-house training to entry level coders. They offer a 3-5 week training program in either their Columbia (SC) or Forrest Park (GA) office. If the new hires don't currently have an AHIMA credential, it is required that they obtain it by the end of their training period. Entry level coders must commit to Lexicode for a minimum of 2 years.

Lexicode pays employees an hourly rate plus a productivity incentive plan. They offer good benefits, which include health insurance, a 401k savings plan, paid time off (including holidays), and reimbursement on continuing education.

Maxim Health Information Services hires experienced medical coders. They require applicants to have at least 3 years of experience and have one of the following coding certifications: RHIA, RHIT, CCS,

CCS-P, CPC, or CPC-H. They offer several benefits, which include health insurance (medical, dental, vision), life insurance, a 401k plan, free monthly CEUs, and referral bonuses. Based on employees' reviews, Indeed gives this company 4 out of 5 stars.

Pyramid Healthcare Solutions hires experienced medical coders. They require applicants to have at least 2 years of experience and one of the following certifications: RHIA, RHIT, or CCS. They offer some of the best benefits for a healthcare company in my opinion.

- Medical, Dental, Vision, Life, Short-term/Long-term disability
- Flexible spending accounts + health spending accounts
- Matching 401k
- Paid Holidays and Sick Time; 2 weeks paid vacation (in the 1st yr)
- Tuition reimbursement
- Professional development/Ongoing educational webinars
- Merchant Discounts
- Care 24 Employee Assistance Program
- Paid AHIMA/AAPC Membership Dues
- Annual CEUs
- Sign-on/Retention Bonuses

Based on employees' reviews, Indeed gives this company 4.4 out of 5 stars.

Website Testers

Website usability is important. So, website owners hire companies to conduct website evaluations. Those companies will share a portion of the payment with you for your opinion. Each company has its own hardware and software requirements.

Employers

UserFeel doesn't have any requirements, other than a sample test. The applicant waits between 7 to 60 days to get back their results. Upon the test's results, you will get a rating that will determine if and how often you'll get to do their website usability tests. Testers get paid $10 per test and can earn up to $200 per month. They are paid via Paypal at the end of each week.

User Testing has basic requirements like being 18 years old, have your own computer, screen recording software, complete a 1 page form, and an iPhone, iPad, Android, or Windows Phone (if you're interested in doing mobile tests). Testers get paid $10 per website test and $15 per mobile test. They are paid via Paypal weekly.

Consultants

Employers are hiring more consultants as a way to save money rather than hiring full-time employees. Each industry has its own requirements for licenses, educational backgrounds, and years of work experience. Check with reputable trade associations in your industry to see their educational offerings. Online training and certifications can bolster your resume and your credibility with potential employers.

The best way to get started as a consultant is to apply for consulting jobs. You don't necessarily need to have consulting experience. Employers are more interested to work with you because they lack your industry experience. In some cases, the employer may want to form a long-term business relationship by offering you more business. If you are persistent in your efforts, you will be able to make a full-time income as a consultant within a short period of time.

Employers

ClickNWork hires consultants. The company often has a need for a wide range of consultants that are specialized in a particular industry. They have 2 streams of work, *planned* and *ad hoc*. Most of the work received from clients is *planned*, which means it's reliable since it's a set number of hours weekly or monthly. The rest of the work received is considered *ad hoc*, which means it's erratic and often used to fulfill time-sensitive client assignments. The pay depends on a consultant's experience and the assignment complexity, which can range from $25-$150 an hour. They pay via Paypal or bank account once a month.

Maven allows customers to search the network for experts (or Mavens) to answer their client's professional questions and invite relevant experts to participate in consulting interactions via telephone consultations or electronic surveys. Experts are invited to decide whether if they would be helpful or not. If so, they are compensated for their time.

Experts should work on improving their profile to increase the likelihood of getting more clients for consultations. Experts should set their rate high enough to assure clients that the received information is thorough, professional, and being purchased at a competitive price. However, Maven is a marketplace and clients will compare prices between Mavens to obtain the best quality service at the best price.

Maven pays experts via Paypal, electronic funds transfer (ACH), bank wire transfer, or by check. It takes 7-10 days from your request to receive payment.

Whether you want to focus on a specific niche or do a combination of niches, there is no doubt that you can make a full-time income working from home and do it for the rest of your life. The employers discussed in this chapter do not reflect a complete list of work from home opportunities. However, this is a good list to get you started.

CHAPTER 11

Make A 6 Figure Salary In Real Estate Without A License Or Prior Experience

We are involved in real estate in some form. Some people use real estate simply for housing purposes, whether they're leasing or becoming a homeowner. Some people use real estate as an investment vehicle, whether they're investing in tax liens, rental properties, or buy and hold properties. Other people use real estate as a profession. The majority of professionals in the real estate industry are realtors. However, there are many other real estate careers that are available to the public.

Most people who are eager to get started in the real estate industry take the traditional route, which is taking courses at a college or university. At several institutions, students can specialize in a niche that can lead to obtaining a real estate certificate or degree. Most people start in real estate as a realtor or an office assistant for a company that is directly involved in real estate or has relations to it. While some companies offer advancement opportunities to their current staff, it is not guaranteed that they can reach their desired level of status within their ideal timeframe.

I think most people are not concerned about their career status if they are earning their ideal salary. Who cares about being vice president of a real estate firm if you are earning $100,000 a year as a wholesaler? How about we skip the formal education and only leave you with the information that will make you successful? I bet you would prefer that route. There is nothing wrong with courses offered by higher education institutions. I'm quite sure that those students can find some value in them. However, I chose to learn from a few seasoned professionals to build my real estate empire.

So, are you ready to make a 6 figure salary in real estate without a type of license or prior experience? The things that you will learn in this chapter are not particularly common knowledge in the real estate industry. Sometimes, when I talk to realtors or real estate brokers about some of my real estate strategies, they look at me like I'm from another planet. This is the ignorance that keeps real estate investors (including myself) ahead of the game.

Some people would argue that there is a conspiracy orchestrated by the National Association of Realtors. Some people believe that the NAR indoctrinates their professionals in a model that creates dependency within their system. This theory is quite plausible and can explain why some real estate investors choose to separate themselves from the NAR altogether. Below are a few statements made by different realtors about the topic in a discussion on Trulia (titled "*Is the Realtor brand a national conspiracy that restricts free trade, desecrates anti-trust laws, and plunders its members?*").

"I believe the "Realtor" brand and the NAR is a "conspiracy" to infuse the profession with a code of conduct and ethical behavior."

—**Margo Currie** (Exit 1 Stop Realty)

"The NAR boasts about ethics, yet they are proven liars and manipulators of housing data."

—**Fred Griffin** (Your Real Estate Broker of Tallahassee)

"We ... need an organization that upholds and promotes our collective professional image. NAR has proved that it is not the organization that will deliver."

—**E.J. Carlier** (Century 21 MarketLink Realty)

"The NAR admitted that they've lost nearly 300 thousand members already which equates to an annual revenue loss of 24 million bucks. Thousands of real estate agents are looking for non-affiliated brokerages. Thousands will continue to seek shelter under the umbrella of non-affiliation."

—**David Saks** (The Real Estate Mart of Tennessee)

"I have to agree, it may be time for NAR to go away. They don't protect us or help us. They have become a political organization lobbying the government with our money, whether we agree with their efforts or not."

—**Sandra Paulow** (Aspen Properties Inc)

In 2008, there was a lawsuit between the United States and the NAR regarding Internet based brokers. The Anti-Trust Division challenged the NAR's MLS rules that inhibited competition from internet based brokers. On November in that same year, the court made a judgment that approved a settlement against the NAR. The final judgment ordered the NAR to repeal the policies challenged by the U.S. and replace those policies with rules that do not discriminate against innovative brokers. Now, do you understand why some real estate investors and entities prefer to have no relations with the NAR?

Please don't think that I have something against members of the NAR. I work with some real estate agents who are NAR members because they play an instrumental role in my business. They are not the problem. The management team is the problem. I am so thankful to live in a country that maintains a system of "checks and balances." They keep organizations like the NAR from controlling the free market, which gives both individuals and entities a level playing field.

So, we talked about the most common route that people pursue regarding a real estate career, which can be profitable and enjoyable. However, I find it to be lackluster compared to the other route, also known as the "real estate investor." Real estate investors are typically involved in wholesale transactions, rehab projects, tax liens, and creative financing. There are many niches in real estate investing which allows people to discover where their talents are suited best.

The best way to get started in real estate is to be a property scout (also known as a bird dog). The term "*bird dog*" comes from the name of the animal who hunts to retrieve birds or other small game animals by tracking their scent. People who don't know about the animal are likely to be unaware of the term and its relation to real estate. So, from here on, I would continue to refer to this position as property scout. I feel that this is the best way for any novice to learn and gain real estate experience. You don't need any money, credit, or experience to get started.

The first thing that a property scout needs to consider is their desired specialization regarding property. On the most basic level, there is residential and commercial real estate. Residential real estate is usually property that people call home while commercial real estate is property typically used for business. The next step is to find your niche, whether it's in residential or commercial. In commercial real estate, a person can specialize in land or buildings. In residential real estate, a person can specialize in land, single family homes and multi-family homes. As a property scout, you may work for a real estate company or a seasoned real estate investor. It is likely that most property scouts will start with single family homes since it appears to be the most common specialization for real estate investors.

The second thing that a property scout needs to consider is their city limits. This part may be up to the investor since they will be paying you in the end. They will likely give you a criterion, based on their investing preferences. However, there are investors who are liberal in their approach. Liberal investors may give you more freedom to specialize in a suburb, city, or neighborhood. I would highly recommend for any new property scout to be a micro-specialist.

Let's say that you are a new property scout living in Austin, Texas. I wouldn't recommend trying to cover the Austin metropolitan area nor would I recommend covering the entire city of Austin only. You need to specialize on the micro level! Focus on specializing in a certain part of the city like Southwest Austin or Northwest Austin. Once you have picked an area, study the neighborhoods within that area. How diverse is the neighborhood? Are there good schools in the area? Do residents need to drive long distances to do major shopping? Does the neighborhood have public transit in the area? What is the average resident's income? What are the age demographics? As a micro-specialist, you want to be the expert regarding your area. So, learn as much as you can about your target area because it will pay off in huge amounts down the road.

The third thing that a property scout needs to consider is their ability to build rapport. One good way to build rapport is to attend city council meetings. Attending these meetings regularly is a good way to get information and build rapport indirectly. Some other ways that a property scout can stay informed is by attending chamber of commerce groups, civic based organizations, and special interest groups (i.e. meetup.com). Being active in these groups can provide you access to potential buyers and investors. As an added bonus, you can form some great relationships and enhance your reputation and integrity among the community.

Now that we're all done with the considerations, let's talk about how the property scout gets paid from the real estate investor. Most real estate investors have access to the MLS (or multiple listing service), which shows all of the real estate listings in that city. Since the real estate investor has access to this resource, you would not help them by sending them listings that are already posted there. However, you would help them by bringing properties that are not listed on the MLS. These properties may be abandoned, vacant, or for sale by owner.

Property scouts are paid $5-$15 for each lead generated and receive a $500-$1000 bonus on any deals that are bought by the real estate investor. Some real estate investors may not pay for any leads but only for the properties that they bought from the property scout's list. The latter form of payment is deemed illegal in some states. It is good to have a contractual agreement between yourself and the real estate investor for legal reasons. Property scouts don't make as much as wholesalers because they don't talk with the owner to negotiate the deal. However, being a property scout is a good prerequisite to being a wholesaler.

Once you have become a successful property scout, you are fully qualified to become a wholesaler. There are a lot of similarities between a property scout and a wholesaler. Like property scouts, wholesalers don't need any money, credit, or experience either. A wholesaler will be better prepared if they have prior experience as a property scout. However, it is not necessary to become a wholesaler. The difference between a property scout and a wholesaler is the involvement in the transaction. While the property scout only qualifies and sends unlisted leads, the wholesaler usually does the tasks of a property scout and negotiates the purchase price with the homeowner to reach an agreement.

Including the knowledge that is obtained as a property scout, there are a few more things that a person needs to know to be a wholesaler. An effective marketing budget is the most important thing that will make or break a wholesaler. The best way to optimize your marketing expenses is to employ some low cost methods (which can be just as effective as high cost methods) and generate more business from your previous customers. We all want to maximize our profits from each transaction. However, it is hard for a person to do it when their marketing expenses are eating away at their profits. It wouldn't be very profitable for a transaction to yield me $2000 (in profit) minus $700 (for marketing expenses), using 13 hours of my time. Some people may find it quite profitable. Even with the high marketing cost for one transaction, the wholesaler still earns $1300 (or $100/hr for 13 hours). However, the most important question of all is asking yourself: "What is your time worth?" At one point of my life, I would have been quite satisfied with the $1300 profit. After several years later, I no longer find those types of transactions worth my time.

There are many types of marketing that a wholesaler can use in their business. There is online and offline marketing. Today, we live in the Information Age where online marketing has become the preferred way for lead generation. I like some of the free online methods like classified websites, video marketing, and article submission websites.

Craigslist is the most popular *classified website* and it's free to post ads in most cities. I use Craigslist in conjunction with Postlets and/ or VFlyer to create the most attractive ads. The lesser known classified websites are Backpage and EBay Classifieds. If you are low on marketing funds, posting your real estate deals there may be worthwhile since there are no marketing costs involved. There are at least 5 other free classified websites that are lesser known than Backpage and EBay Classifieds.

These free classified websites are included if you are using Postlets or VFlyer syndication.

Video marketing is another great form of online marketing but it may be at a learning curve for some people. Before you create any video for your real estate YouTube channel, it is important to clarify the intent of your video. Let's say that you have a property for sale. You can record the video with a mini-cam, providing a virtual tour to your viewers. When you come to the end of the virtual tour, you can add a "call to action" by encouraging viewers to visit your website for more details.

Regarding websites, you don't have to spend a lot of money to get a decent website. There are blog platforms like WordPress and Blogger that includes free software tools to enhance the functionality of your website. The only other thing that will be required is your domain name. In order to present yourself to your audience as a real business, it is important to get your own domain name rather than using the WordPress or Blogger subdomain.

The last free method that is worth mentioning is *article submission websites*. These sites are great for building content in their article library as their brand lends credibility to your business. Creating articles is not hard at all. If you have any internet research skills, you can take bits of information and turn them into 500 word articles. Most of these article submission sites have a resource box intact, which is included at the end of your articles. The resource box allows you to include your personal and business profile, and links to your website or social media pages. The premier article site is EzineArticles. One of their guidelines is that all articles are to be informational only (no selling or promoting) with no links in the body of the article. Other article submission sites like GoArticles and ArticleDashboard allow links within the body of the article.

While online marketing allows you to reach a wider audience than offline marketing, it is also possible to concentrate on smaller target areas by using paid online marketing methods. There are numerous online marketing methods that are quite affordable but I will only mention the most popular and effective ones.

Google Adwords are those sponsored ads that appear on the right of the Google search results. These ads are highly targeted based on keywords and the customer doesn't pay for anything unless the ad(s) are clicked (also known as pay per click).

Pay per click ads can increase site visits by 17% and sales by 136%. Purchases that were influenced by PPC ads had a 21% higher average sale than those that weren't influenced by PPC. Both online orders and buyers per visitor fell by 23% percent when PPC ads were stopped. So, what are the takeaways from all of this data? PPC can increase site visitors but more importantly increase sales. Site visitors derived from PPC ads convert better and more valuable than non-PPC visitors from revenue per sale standpoint.

Facebook ads are those sponsored ads appear on the right of the Facebook Wall. The mechanics of these ads are somewhat similar to Google Adwords. A lot of big name brands have employed Facebook as a means of advertising. The following companies have had success with their advertising:

1800 Flowers used their ads to give fans 15% of their purchase and 50 credits to be used for Facebook Games. They implemented "shared stories" that allowed friends of consumers to see their purchases. The results were amazing. The company doubled their page's fans to over 120,000 fans. The campaign increased engagement on their page and 4,000 transactions occurred as a direct result of the Facebook Credits offer.

20ᵗʰ Century Fox wanted to acquire a mass of fans on the film's (Wall Street - Money Never Sleeps) Facebook page. Fox wanted to appeal to the older audiences who saw the original movie and the younger audiences who were eager to see the modern version. The results were good. A tracking study found more than 1.1 million people had intended on seeing the movie after seeing their Facebook ads, while over a quarter of pollsters that left the movie remembered seeing the Facebook ads. More than 260,000 people liked the page.

Ace Hardware noted that their busiest season is arriving and wanted to increase their fans and create an online presence for their brand. The company decided to advertise discounts to their fans. They also targeted people with home maintenance and repair keywords in their profiles. The results were phenomenal. In 4 days, their page went from 20,000 fans to nearly 50,000 fans. The campaign generated almost 50,000 clicks to the Facebook page and the number of fan postings on the page grew by 900%.

Adidas wanted to increase the number of fans (especially 18-34 year olds) on its Facebook page, encourage video engagement, and re-introduce itself as a trendy fashion brand. The campaign was successful. They had a 6% increase in Facebook fans and their video ads resulted in over 722,000 engagements.

American Express recently aimed at assisting small businesses through their "Small Business Saturday" (a day when Americans shop at local stores and not at large corporations). The results were quite impressive. 47% of people who saw the company's efforts on Facebook had a more favorable impression of the company. The company's Facebook page gained over 1.4 million fans and more than 100,000 small business owners downloaded promotional materials from the Facebook page.

AT&T looked to its Facebook page to increase customer relations. Using 3 different campaigns, they received several confirmations about their brand and quality of service. AT&T found through surveys that the company goes above and beyond on their service. The perceptions of their brand are better in their Facebook community than anywhere else.

Bob Evans wanted to increase its Facebook fan base and promote its National French Fries Day. The campaign was successful. They garnered 84+ million impressions, 21,000+ clicks, and 12,000 likes (and 5,000 more a week after the campaign).

Budweiser wanted to connect with their fans worldwide during the 2010 World Cup. The results were phenomenal. During the event, their Facebook page received 900,000+ visitors, which gained them 6 fans per minute.

Carnival wanted to increase its engagements on Facebook by promoting 2 of their sweepstakes and their new cruise ship, Carnival Magic. With the Facebook campaign, the company was able to set the record of being the first cruise company to reach 1 million fans. Nearly one-third (370,000) of their fan base has came directly from Facebook ads. Over half of their fans visit the page daily.

Cheerios wanted to connect with their main demographic, mothers with young children. The company promised to donate a free book to First Book (a charity that gives books to needy children) for every new fan. The results were amazing. The Cheerios' Facebook page increased 1500% by going from nearly 9,000 fans to 130,000+ fans.

Pedigree wanted to raise awareness about the 4 million dogs living in shelters, help raise donations for those dogs, and create a place online to unite dog lovers. The campaign was a great success. Their Facebook page went from 55,000 fans to 1.1+ million fans and was able to raise $600,000 for animal shelters nationwide.

P.F. Chang wanted to celebrate its 18th anniversary by offering fans a free coupon of a free lettuce wrap and increase engagement levels. The results were quite impressive. More than 50,000 people redeemed the Facebook coupon and almost half of them were new guests. They increased their page post engagement levels by 3300% and their fan base doubled to 420,000 fans.

Bing ads are those sponsored ads that appear on the right of the Bing search results. While Bing is not as popular as Google, they definitely stand as a rival since they are the superior option in different ways. They cover Bing and Yahoo in 1 place and their ads are cheaper than Google Adwords. Unlike Google, Bing also offers a negative keywords conflict report, which tells you what negative keywords are causing you to exclude wanted traffic.

Then, there is offline marketing. While online marketing is the more popular choice, offline marketing is still used quite often in most businesses. There are several free offline methods that are quite effective like farming the area, searching newspapers for leads, cold calling, and door knocking.

The first method is *farming the area*, which is recording addresses of distressed properties in your target market. You would then do your due diligence to see the status regarding those properties. If the property is not an active MLS listing or already under contract with another party, it is quite likely that you may found a motivated seller.

The second method is *searching newspapers for leads*. This is a method that tends to get overlooked quite a bit. A lot of people assume that the newspapers are slowly dying and no one reads them anymore. This is not true at all. Senior citizens are likely to read newspapers and post ads there than any other age group. There is an abundance of leads in newspapers. Death notices (or obituaries), for sale by owner (FSBO), public auctions, foreclosures, and divorce settlements are all types of leads that can be found in newspapers.

The third method is *cold calling*, which is quite an effective technique since most rookie wholesalers shy away from this method. I think a lot of novices make it more intimidating than it appears. What's the worst thing that can happen from cold calling? The worst thing that can happen is the homeowner turning down your offer or hanging up on you. Your success of cold calling is based on the law of averages (more phone calls = more deals). The only challenge that you may find is overcoming rejection. Please keep in mind that you probably will never see these people again in your life. Who cares if a few people were annoyed by your phone call? If a homeowner doesn't request to not be contacted again, I will contact them in the future to see if things have changed. More often than not, wholesalers will trash leads after being turned down on the first time. A third up to an half of my leads is contacting homeowners that I have contacted in the past. There are only 2 exceptions in where I would trash leads, if the property has been sold (by me hopefully or someone else) or the homeowner has requested not to be contacted again.

The last free offline marketing method that I will mention is *door knocking*. If you have absolutely no money but have a lot of time, door knocking may be an effective marketing strategy for you. It is the most time-consuming of all the techniques out there and one of the most effective since most wholesalers avoid it. Bring out a lot of business cards with you because you will need something tangible to leave behind if they are not home. If you are new to door knocking, it may be helpful to bring along a companion to ease some tension. Companions of the opposite sex work well because it makes the homeowner more comfortable, which will double the chances of your offer being accepted. Be sure to track your progress with a map or an Excel spreadsheet of your intended addresses.

If you have some money for marketing, there are several paid offline methods that are quite effective and affordable like bandit signs, direct mail, and billboards.

Bandit signs are probably the best bang for your buck in my opinion. They are those yellow or white signs that you see nailed on telephone poles. Some of those signs read "We Buy Houses, Fast + Cash, 212-555-1234." You don't need a lot of tools to form your own bandit signs. The only materials that you'll need are a black marker (preferably a

Sharpie Magnum), blank white or yellow corrugated signs, roofing nails, and a hammer. There is typically no learning curve to make a bandit sign. However, there are countless YouTube videos if you need assistance. Please keep in mind that bandit signs do not work in every city. If you do not see any bandit signs in your area, it is likely that they aren't welcomed there. Some cities have vigilant code enforcement, which means that you can face fines and your signs may not last more than 1-2 days.

Direct mail is one of the oldest yet effective forms of offline marketing. The most common forms of direct mail are yellow letters and postcards. What are yellow letters? It is a handwritten letter written on a yellow legal pad paper. The response rate is typically between 5-15% and that's quite good when you consider that it only takes 1 deal to make it worthwhile. The biggest problem with direct mail is that it doesn't get opened. People will always give it something more attention if it is personalized. If someone sent you a handwritten letter, would you open it? After all, you're probably curious about the contents of the letter. Once the letter is read, the reader feels compelled to contact you, which increases the likelihood of getting a response. So, what about postcards? While they are not as effective as yellow letters, it is better used for a general mass mailing campaign. Postcards are the informal option to yellow letters. I use yellow letters for probates, inheritances, evictions, bankruptcies, and divorces since they are usually the higher quality leads. By making the best impression possible, I increase my chances of getting a response from them.

Billboards are commonly seen as advertisements on highways and principal streets but they also come in other forms. Digital billboards are somewhat different from their conventional counterparts. They are designed to display running text, display several different ads, or even provide several companies with different time slots. Mobile billboards can be found at bus stops, train stations, airports, and sports arenas.

They also can be found on buses, trains, taxi cabs, and pedicabs. These billboards are the most convenient since they can be moved as needed. While all of the marketing methods mentioned are affordable for most people, billboards are definitely the most expensive method. Some people may worry about whether it's a good investment since they don't know how to track leads coming from billboard advertisements. If you employ multiple forms of marketing, then there are several ways that can distinguish whether your leads are coming from your billboards. One way to measure your ROI is by using another website domain. This alternate domain will separate your billboard traffic from your other web traffic. Another way is by using a unique coupon code in your billboard advertisement, which can help you distinguish between regular web traffic and billboard traffic.

So, there are many types of marketing that a wholesaler can use in their business, based on their budget. Once you have developed a marketing plan, the next suggested step is to look for the investors (or cash buyers) that will be purchasing your deals. The best way to find these cash buyers are at real estate investor association (better known as REIA) meetings. At these meetings, you can find buy and hold investors, rehabbers, and other vendors that could possibly be interested in your deals. While REIAs are a great way to meet cash buyers, you can also meet them outside of REIAs. Do you know somebody that would be interested in your deals? It could be your former high school teacher, college professor, supervisor, doctor, or lawyer. Think about the people that you interact with on a daily to monthly basis. A lot of these people that you know may go through the traditional process of shopping for a home. If you approach them with your deals, they may be likely to consider your offers since the price will be below fair market value (FMV). Seasoned cash buyers tend to have their own criteria of desired properties, while casual cash buyers are not as selective.

The next important tool for wholesalers is to have a sales aptitude. This aptitude is the bridge that can turn leads into profits. I feel that the best way to develop this skill is through experience. My best recommendation in developing this skill is to get a sales job that offers a base pay plus commission. For relevancy, it would be ideal to find a sales job in the real estate industry. Leasing consultants and mortgage professionals are some good entry level careers. It would be wise to be committed to the position for at least a year or until you're confident to proceed as a wholesaler. Some people opt to avoid that route by accepting the learning curve of being a successful salesperson and practice by talking and negotiating with homeowners. It's not a bad route but it can be discouraging to people who aren't patient.

Once you have developed your sales aptitude, you will need the contracts to complete your transactions. Wholesalers typically use the same 2 contracts for all of their deals. The first contract is the purchase agreement, which executes the sale of real estate between the wholesaler (you) and the homeowner. The second contract is the assignment of agreement, which assigns your rights in the initial purchase agreement to an investor (or cash buyer).

Cash buyers can be great business partners or sticklers. When a wholesaler uses an assignment of agreement, the document reveals the wholesaler's profit. Some cash buyers do not mind honoring your profit margin because they are still getting a good deal. However, there are some cash buyers who may gripe about your profit. Sometimes, they will belittle you by stating that you didn't do a lot of work to justify such a profit. They will try to talk you down to a price that makes them feel more comfortable. I will never advise walking away from money to win a battle. Take the money and let these people be the last for consideration of your future deals. Once you know who the sticklers are, it would be smart to go for the other option discussed in the next paragraph.

Sometimes, wholesalers will just use 2 purchase agreements to execute the deal. Wholesalers may prefer this option when they want their profit hidden in the deal. This option is commonly known as a double closing. For example, let's say that John Boy (the wholesaler) successfully reached a deal with Homer (the homeowner) and wants to wholesale it for a profit. John Boy got a house that is worth $200k for $100k and intends to make $15k off of the property. This is the A (aka the homeowner) to B (aka the wholesaler) transaction. John Boy now has that signed agreement and will take another purchase agreement with his $15k profit included in the purchase price to Joe (the investor). This is the B (aka the wholesaler) to C (aka the investor). At that point, both contracts are taken to the title company. Once both transactions are executed, all parties are satisfied. Homer walks away with his $100k. Joe walks away with the title of a $200k property for $115k. And John Boy walks away with his profit of $15k. That's the mechanics of wholesaling. The wholesaler gets paid by including their profit in each deal.

The final stage in wholesaling is to have an investor friendly title company. As mentioned in the previous paragraph, the title companies are the entities that will be closing your deals. Every title company does not understand wholesaling. Some of them think that it's illegal. If you don't believe me, see for yourself. I would rather save you the time though. Refer to your local REIA about investor friendly title companies in your area. I would recommend you to develop a good rapport with them. After all, they will be handing you the paycheck.

Once you have become a successful wholesaler, you are fully qualified to become a rehabber. Rehabbers make up a third to half of the cash buyers that buy wholesale deals. So, it would be prudent to become a great wholesaler first in order to recognize good deals from wholesalers as a rehabber. I know there are some ambitious people that want to take the shortcut to success. However, there is a lot of required education in order for a person to be a successful rehabber. Being a wholesaler is a good prerequisite to being a rehabber. If you are not patient and want to jump right in, I would advise to shadow a successful rehabber. Sometimes, these seasoned rehabbers may offer training courses. Or why not befriend a successful rehabber at your local REIA? "When there is a will, there is a way." If you are persistent in being a rehabber, you'll eventually find a rehabber that will teach you the business.

The most important thing that a rehabber needs is funding. If you don't have a secure form of funding, then you need to work on securing a form of funding. A secure form of funding can be funds from a loan, a private or hard money lender, or money from a bank account (401k, IRA, CD, or savings account). I would suggest working on having multiple options of funding. What if you don't have any money? Then, your options would be limited to private and hard money lenders. What is the difference between a private and hard money lender? Private money lenders can be anyone who is likely to loan money on negotiable terms. Hard money lenders are finance professionals who loan money on non-negotiable terms. They already have their own lending criteria, which include the loan duration, interest rate, and upfront points. While private money is more flexible and cheaper, hard money is usually more abundant. Why is it the case? Well, private money lenders are usually not advertising that they're lending money. They may be happy to invest but this is not their profession. On the other hand, hard money lenders often advertise because they are specifically in the lending business.

Once you have secured funding, you will need the deals to fund. While rehabbers are in the business of rehabilitating homes, they would prefer the deals that don't require any renovations. Although rehabbers don't mind fix and flip projects, deals that require minimal work to cure a property are preferable. Their goal in every deal is to use the minimum amount of funds for rehabilitation and sell the property for the maximum profit.

Let's look at a hypothetical example. A Philadelphia property has a fair market value of $230k. The rehabber bought the deal from a wholesaler for $145k. The property needs $20k in repairs, bringing the rehabber's balance to $165k. The house has been fully rehabilitated and now for sale at $215k. The gross profit from the deal is 50k minus expenses (paying independent contractors, etc). Surely, the rehabber could have sold it for the fair market price but this decision varies based on current market conditions. If it is a fast growing city and housing options are slim, then selling it at full price is justified. Otherwise, selling it below fair market value is a more attractive sale since prospective buyers like to feel that they are getting a good deal.

Before starting any rehab project, it is important for the rehabber to hire competent workers to produce the best property rehabilitation possible. Sometimes, new rehabbers get excited about the potential profits and hire cheap labor to maximize their profit margins. Do not let profit margins cloud your judgment in quality. There is an old adage that says "Do it right the first time." The adage will forever hold its weight. Be selective in who you recruit to be part of your rehab team. I would recommend starting with people that you may already know. You may have a neighbor who uses the same electrician or carpenter. Begin searching within your network. It could be much easier looking within your network than outside your network. However, if you don't have a network, look for local contractors and interview them. Request that they show you some picture galleries of their previous projects. Ask for their previous clients' contact information to get opinions about the contractor. Once you have interviewed all of the prospects, you will be able to make an informed decision about who you will hire on to your team.

There is another option in finding a great rehab team. Instead of hiring people individually, you may want to consider in hiring a general contractor or project manager. A general contractor will typically hire subcontractors for 80-90% of the rehabber's payment and keep the difference as their fee. A general contractor can save you time because you don't have to recruit contractors individually. An alternative to a general contractor is hiring a project manager. Technical colleges are a good place to start looking for project managers. They can be electricians, carpenters, or any technical profession related in a home rehabilitation project. As a licensed professional, they typically have friends and/or colleagues in the home improvement industry. The project manager will hire their own team, manage the project, and pay the subcontractors like a general contractor. They are not usually very experienced but their academic knowledge makes for a useful tool. If your budget is accommodating, it can be a good idea to hire a project manager on a full-time basis (given you have enough projects to keep them busy).

The last thing that a rehabber needs to consider is how they will pay the general contractor or project manager. The most common form of payment is a flat fee. The rehabber pays a flat fee when the project is completed as promised. The second most common form of payment is a flat fee with performance bonuses. The rehabber pays performances bonuses when budgets and deadlines are met on top of the flat fee for the project. The last and less popular form of payment is a percentage of the profits. The rehabber pays a small percentage of the profits to the general contractor or project manager. The general rule to this form of payment is that the rehabber pays up to 20% of the profits made on the deal. For example, let's use the same hypothetical example regarding the Philadelphia property mentioned earlier, which yielded the rehabber a $50k profit. Instead of paying the common flat fee, the rehabber will pay 10-20% (or $5-10k) to the general contractor or project manager. I would personally pay the project manager (10-15%) and the general contractor (15-20%). After all, the general contractor is much likely to have more experience than the project manager. The only caveat to this form of payment is that the rehab team doesn't get paid until the property is sold. As a rehabber, I wouldn't recommend this form of payment in a depressed real estate market. It may take years to pay the rehab team if you're waiting to pay them from the profits made on the sale of the property.

So, we talked about some of the active real estate strategies. Do you prefer a more "hands off" approach to real estate investing? Perhaps, you don't want to deal with homeowners, tenants, contractors, and/ or other real estate investors. Let's talk about some of the passive real estate strategies like tax liens, buy and hold investing, and private money lending.

What is a buy and hold investor? A buy and hold investor is a person that buys real estate and holds on to it for a long time. This tactic is based on the view that the real estate market will provide a good rate of return in the long term. Some of the wealthiest people in the world amassed their great fortunes through buy and hold investing. These buy and hold investors typically rent out their properties. Owning multiple properties all producing monthly cash flow is a great way to build a reliable stream of income. The buy and hold investor will sell at some point but they prefer to wait for ideal market appreciation.

For example, if they originally bought a property for $100k, they may prefer to wait until it's worth $300k. Whether it takes 10 or 20 years for the appreciation to come to that amount, the buy and hold investor is patient because they still benefit from the monthly cash flow. When their property has appreciated to their ideal amount, they will put their house up for sale in order to cash out. Once they have cashed out, they may opt for the capital gains (also known as the profit) or invest the profits into a similar property through a 1031 exchange. What's the difference between the two? Capital gains are subject to taxation, whereas a 1031 exchange defers capital gains taxes until the property is sold. You can still profit from a 1031 exchange after the sale of the initial property. I will discuss that strategy more in the later chapter.

If you choose the buy and hold route, you won't have to worry about dealing with contractors because buy and hold investors are likely to buy properties in excellent condition. The only challenges that you may encounter are dealing with homeowners for price negotiation as well as dealing with tenants. Tenants are going to be the most challenging between the two but you can totally avoid the headache by outsourcing it to someone else for a flat fee.

The next passive strategy that I will discuss is private money lending. I discussed it earlier in this chapter. Now, I will talk about how you can be a private money lender. There are 2 ways to do it successfully. Before we talk about it those ways, it's important to have your documents in place when conducting this type of business. Some documents that you want to consider are a promissory note contract, terms of agreement contract, and a prospectus. A prospectus is important because it informs potential investors about the features of the business deal. It serves as a great filter because certain people may not qualify or be comfortable with your terms. The terms of agreement contract revisits the terms outlined in the prospectus and elaborates on all of the details involved. The promissory note is another level of assurance that the borrower will satisfy his financial obligations. The borrower usually provides some form of collateral that is equivalent to the value of the loan to exemplify confidence to the lender. Any person who isn't willing to put collateral or a significant amount of their money in the deal should not be considered. Before you consider making any loan, interview the person and ask for references to ensure that you're dealing with a seasoned professional. Go over each investment deal several times to ensure that it's a good deal.

Now, let's talk about the 2 different ways to be a successful private money lender. The first way is by using your own money. If you already have thousands of dollars in your reserves, then you can be the direct lender. This is the easier way. The other way is by using other people's money. If you have done several deals using private money lenders and have at least 3 reliable lenders, you can charge rates that are higher than your lenders'. You will be leveraging your lender's money to make loans to clients. For example, you have 3 private money lenders that you deem reliable. One lender charges 4%, another lender charge 6% and the other lender charges 7%. If you set your rate at 10%, you can earn between 3-6% on your money. As a private money lender, you are the bank to most investors who don't qualify for a traditional loan. That's quite a good position to be in if you ask me.

Another passive strategy is tax liens. What are tax liens? A tax lien is a paper certificate that is placed on a property by the government when the owner fails to pay their property taxes. Those liens are sold to private investors and almost $6 billion liens come up for sale annually. When tax liens are executed, the local government gets their money immediately and the buyer of the tax lien gets the right to collect the delinquent tax (a penalty and interest on the late payment that can be as high as 36% a year, depending on the state). While tax liens are not available in every state, these liens can be found in the following U.S. states and territories: Alabama, Arizona, Colorado, Florida, Illinois, Indiana, Iowa, Kentucky, Louisiana, Maryland, Mississippi, Missouri, Montana, Nebraska, Nevada, New Jersey, New York, Ohio, Pennsylvania, Puerto Rico, South Carolina, U.S. Virgin Islands, Vermont, Washington DC, West Virginia, and Wyoming. There are several advantages to investing in tax liens. One advantage is the amount of capital required to get started. If you have as little as $50, you can invest in tax liens. Another advantage is the low risk involved in these investments. While tax liens may contain risks associated with municipal fines, bankruptcy, and government errors, they are still lower in risk profile than other investments. Why settle for 1-3% interest in a CD or savings account when you can average between 10-36% interest by investing in tax liens? This is probably the most passive and "hands off" approach to real estate investing. No need to worry about tenants, contractors, or homeowners. The local government runs the whole process and is there to assist you with any problems. More or less, the government is your business partner since you both have a vested interest.

Earlier in this chapter, I talked about alternative funding sources (or creative financing) like private and hard money loans. Creative financing certainly isn't limited to those 2 options. There are several other options like FHA loans, 203K loans, seller financing, partnerships, and IRAs.

Let's begin by talking about FHA loans. What is a FHA loan? It is a government insured mortgage loan that was created to make loans accessible and affordable. It offers a low down payment of 3.5% and accepts applicants with less than perfect credit. Even if you had a bankruptcy or lost due to foreclosure, you may still be able to qualify for the loan. There are maximum mortgage limits for FHA loans that vary by state and county. In certain counties, you may be able to get financing for a loan size up to $729,750. Although there is a rule requiring the homeowner to live in the property, the homeowner can still rent out the other units if it's a multifamily property. Another advantage of a FHA loan is that it can be assignable (meaning if you wanted to sell your home, you can "assign" your FHA loan to the buyer). So, it would make it an attractive sale to sell it as a cash flow property rather than a traditional, non-performing property.

There is a derivative of the FHA loan called the 203K loan. It's a loan given to buyers who want to buy a damaged or older home to do repairs on it. Usually, this loan also includes up to a 20% "contingency reserve" (which grants additional funds if the repair costs end up costing more than the suggested estimates) and up to 6 months of mortgage payments included to allow the homeowner to live elsewhere during the renovation period. However, there are 2 types of 203k mortgage loans: regular and streamlined. With a regular 203k loan, the maximum amount that you can get is the lesser of these 2 amounts: the as-is value of the property plus repairs or 110% of the estimated value of the property after repairs. With a streamlined loan, you can get a loan for the purchase price of the home plus up to $35,000. In this situation, I would recommend in getting the FHA to cover as many mortgage payments as possible. Shortly before the rehab project is completed, I would start marketing the property looking for tenants for 1 year leases. Once all of the units are leased, I would start marketing the property for sale a month prior to the loan's anniversary. After the sale of the property, I will walk away with 6-9 months of rental payments from 2-4 units and a 20-50% markup on the fair market value price (since the property is a cash flowing asset). Then, I will take those capital gains to invest it into another property through a 1031 exchange (which will defer my tax liability). Once the 1031 exchange is executed, I will get the property to cash flow and then sell the cash flowing property on a seller financing deal, which is the next creative financing strategy that will be discussed.

What exactly is seller financing? Seller financing is when the seller finances the payments instead of the bank. The criteria of seller financing varies depending on the seller's requirements. While there is seller financing options that can be almost as strict as conventional financing, most of these options are much more flexible than conventional financing. This type of financing offers a lower down payment and lower monthly payments at a fixed interest rate. There are several types of seller financing, which is not limited to a lease option, land contract, or "subject to." However, I will discuss those 3 variants since they are the more popular methods used.

So, what is a lease option? A lease option is when the seller rents the property to a tenant while also giving them the right to buy it within a specified period of time. The tenant benefits by having a fixed purchase price of the property while they work on their loan qualifications for a mortgage. The seller benefits by profiting in 3 different ways. The first way is in the form of the option deposit (1-5% of the purchase price).

Tenants are required to pay an option deposit in order to have "the right to buy" the property at the fixed purchase price. The second way is in the form of monthly rental payments. The tenant's monthly rental payments also include rent credits, which is used towards the purchase price when the tenant is ready to buy the property. The third way is the profit made on the sale of the property. The seller profits by receiving the remaining funds of the sold property when the title transfer has been executed.

Let's look at a hypothetical example. A Cleveland property has a fair market value of $175k. The homeowner sells it to the tenant for $200k on a 2 year lease option contract. The tenant accepts the markup price because he doesn't qualify for a mortgage elsewhere. He gives the homeowner $10k as his option deposit. The total monthly rent is $1000 (which includes a $200/month in rent credits). At the end of 2 years, the tenant has accrued $4800 in rent credits and already has $10k invested as their option deposit. The tenant has been approved for a mortgage of the remaining balance of $185,200. The mortgage company cuts you a check and the deal is complete. All parties are satisfied.

One common objection that I get from real estate novices is "the only problem is that I don't own a property to execute a lease option." What most real estate novices don't know is that you don't need to own property to do lease options. In the words of David Rockefeller, "The secret of success is to own nothing but control everything." How does a person control a property if they don't own it? Contracts! Contracts are what give individuals or corporations control over property. There are option contracts that allow you to look for tenants interested in a lease option and to assign your option to the homeowner for a one-time fee (in cooperative lease options) or by collecting half of all tenant payments (through sandwich lease options). So, whether you own a house or not, you can still make money doing lease options.

So, let's talk about another seller financing variant, which is called the land contract. Sometimes, it is known as a contract for deed or land installment contract. Like lease options, the seller provides financing to the buyer for an agreed purchase price while retaining the legal title to the property. Unlike lease options, the buyer gives the seller a down payment rather than an option deposit. The sale price is paid in monthly installments with the principal and interest fixed into the monthly payment (in lieu of rent credits). The final payment is a large balloon payment that covers the remaining balance owed (as with lease options). Land contracts also allow the buyer to assign their "equitable interest" to another buyer (even if the loan isn't paid in full), which allows the original buyer to sell his equity in the property to a new buyer.

So, how can a real estate investor profit from a land contract? Since land contracts tend to favor the buyer, my recommendation would be to buy the property through a land contract and then sell the same property to a new buyer through a lease option contract. Remember, the buyer in a land contract has equitable interest. You can use this equitable interest to control the property without owning it.

Let's look at a hypothetical example. You buy a Louisville property through a land contract for $200k. The homeowner requires a down payment of $5k. You both agree on a 20 year term at $1500 a month with the last payment being $15k. Now, you can take that same Louisville property and sell it to a buyer through a lease option contract for $215k. You can get a $10k option deposit from the buyer on a 2 year term. The buyer will pay you $1600 a month (including $300/month in rent credits) during the 2 year term. After the 2 year term, the buyer will be expected to pay you the difference through a mortgage. Once the buyer is approved for the mortgage, the mortgage company pays you the difference and then you can satisfy your balance with the original owner of the property. So, you make $5k in the beginning of the deal, $100 a month (totaling $2400) during the 2 year term, and $7,600 at the end. While you can raise the option deposit, purchase price and rental income to increase your profit margins, I wouldn't recommend it because it is very likely that the original owner has already marked up the prices. People may be somewhat desperate to be a homeowner but they're not stupid. If your lease option is not attracting applicants, then you may need to make your terms more realistic to your real estate market.

Another seller financing variant is a "subject to." A "subject to" deal allows you to buy real estate without purchasing it. There are several reasons why a homeowner will give you their house without purchasing it. They may have lost their job and can no longer afford to continue making the payments. They may be going through a divorce and may find it easier to get rid of the property. Their job may be relocating them and they may not have the time to wait for it to be sold. After all, it takes about 3 months to sell a property and then you factor in another month or so to close on the loan.

If the homeowner has little to no equity in the property, they're usually not in a position to sell because agent fees and other costs may be too costly. So, what are their options? Well, they can stop paying their mortgage and lose their home. Or they can sell their home to a real estate investor. The real estate investor may not have all of the cash to make a down payment on the property but that doesn't mean she can't take over the payments. So, the real estate investor would buy the house "subject to" the existing financing, which means the current mortgage stays in tact. She will pay any past due payments to bring the loan current and start sending the monthly payments to their mortgage company. The loan stays in the homeowner's name and the property title is transferred to her name.

One common objection that I hear from real estate novices is the likelihood of triggering the "due on sale" clause. The due on sale clause states that the lien holder can enforce immediate payment of the loan balance if the homeowner sells or transfers any interest of the property to someone else. It is very unlikely that the lender

188 | REACHING THE FINISH LINE

will execute the "due on sale" clause. The mortgage company doesn't care about who's paying the monthly payments. Please remember the job of the lender is to collect the mortgage payments. They loan out money at a higher interest rate that they're paying and create cash flow from the difference on that spread. If a loan is at 9%, why would a lender call that loan due to have it refinanced at a lower interest rate? They would be cutting into their own profit. Do you know of any mortgage companies that like to lose money? I never heard of one and highly doubt you ever did. While it's very unlikely that a lender will execute the "due on sale" clause, there is still a way around it. A land trust holds title to real property and is commonly used by homeowners for tax purposes and estate planning. The homeowner would be the beneficiary and the real estate investor would be the trustee who carries out orders and controls the property. In order to protect your interest in the property, it is important that beneficiary's interest is assigned over to the investor, which will make him the sole owner of the property.

As an investor, there are 3 exit strategies for a "subject to." The first strategy is to rent out the property indefinitely for cash flow. Some investors start with this option because they are not clear on their future intentions regarding the property. The second strategy is to lease option the property. As discussed earlier, this strategy can be a great way to get quick cash upfront, cash flow payments in the middle, and huge lump sum at the end. The third way is to fix and flip the property. The likelihood of an investor profiting is dependent on the property's appreciation in the past few years. Cities that are becoming hot real estate markets are a great environment to use this strategy. Cities that have remained as neutral real estate markets could be a hit or miss for fix and flippers in terms of profiting. Cities that are already depressed or becoming depressed real estate markets, I wouldn't even consider such a strategy. Save yourself the time!

The next creative financing strategy is a partnership. This is not a complicated strategy at all. A real estate investor may lack the experience or financial resources and may call upon a fellow investor to partner up on the deal. Partnerships can be applied to most real estate strategies. Some partnerships may be one-time deals, conducted on an infrequent basis, or through a formal entity like a limited partnership. The shared profits in a partnership are usually 50/50 but those terms can always be negotiated.

Another creative financing strategy that is probably more common nowadays is using your IRA to invest in real estate. While most retirement accounts are subject to an income tax after a withdrawal, you can use the IRA to buy a property. An IRA can legally own real estate and a lot of other investments like precious metals, businesses (excluding S-corporations), foreign currencies, paper assets (stocks, bonds, mutual funds, etc), and commodities. The best IRA for real estate is the Roth IRA. With a Roth, all withdrawals made by you or your heirs are tax free.

So, whichever real estate method that you employ, you can make a 6 figure salary without a license or prior experience. Allow me to illustrate it for you.

Property Scout (Bird Dog)

A seasoned wholesaler offers you an opportunity to work for him. Her terms are the following: She will pay you $500 for every lead that you refer to her, resulting in a successful transaction. You bring her 50 leads every week in which she is able to consistently close on 6 of them (12% conversion rate). (12% is a good conversion rate for real estate sales).

6 successful transactions a week = $3,000 a week

(There are 4.3 weeks in a month)

25 successful transactions a month = $12,500 a month

(There are 12 months in a year)

300 successful transactions a year = $150,000 a year

Tip: Find the best wholesalers in your area and work for them!

Wholesaler

A seasoned rehabber offers you an opportunity to work for him. He is tired of being the wholesaler and the rehabber and would prefer to focus strictly on rehabbing. His terms are the following: He will pay you $5000 for every deal that meets his criteria. You bring him 3 deals every month.

3 deals x $5,000 = $15,000 a month x 12 = $180,000 a year

Tip: Find the rehabbers and/or buy and hold investors with the largest portfolios and work for them!

Rehabber

You have 3 reliable private lenders that offer you attractive interest rates. With this leverage, you could take on as many rehab projects as possible. There is no ceiling to your income. However, you start with the goal of doing 1 rehab project per month with the intent of making $35,000 per deal.

1 deal x $35,000 = $35,000 a month x 12 = $420,000 a year

Tip: Recruit as many lenders as possible. Keep a shortlist of the most reliable lenders. This is the list that you will go to first!

Lease option investor

You decide to invest in lease options because you like the upfront deposit, cash flow in the middle, and huge lump sum in the backend. There is an owner who has a commercial property that is worth $395,000. He's been having a hard time selling it himself and even through a realtor. You approach him to see if he would be interested in doing a lease option. He understands the process and excited to move forward. You both agree to split the option deposit and monthly payments 50/50 and the remaining balance 75/25. You find a great tenant who is in love with the property and meets all of the owner's qualifications. The owner wants $420,000 total (which includes the $24,000 option deposit, $2000 a month for 2 years, and the remaining balance at the end of the term). The tenant happily agrees to the terms and signs the contract. At the end of the term, the tenant exercises their option to buy and pays off the difference with their new mortgage.

Option deposit: $24,000 (50% = $12,000 / your profit)

Monthly payments: $48,000 (50% = $24,000 / your profit)

Remaining balance: $348,000 (25% = $87,000 / your profit)

Your total profit: $123,000

Tip: If you want to earn a six figure profit doing lease options, focus on residential properties in California or commercial properties in cities like Los Angeles, San Francisco, San Diego, New York City, Chicago, Houston, Philadelphia, or Phoenix.

Buy and hold investor

With your high 5 figure income plus the favor that you have with lenders, you have the ability to create or expand your cash flow portfolio. You buy 7 properties in the Los Angeles metropolitan area (4 properties in the suburbs and 6 properties in the city). Your 4 properties in the suburbs cash flow, one at $1000 a month and three at $1400 a month. Your 3 properties in the city cash flow, two at $1200 and one at $1400 a month.

Suburban properties

$1000 a month x 12 = $12,000 a year

$1400 a month x 12 = $16,800 a year

$1400 a month x 12 = $16,800 a year

$1400 a month x 12 = $16,800 a year

City properties

$1200 a month x 12 = $14,400 a year

$1200 a month x 12 = $14,400 a year

$1400 a month x 12 = $16,800 a year

Total cash flow from properties: $108,000 a year

Tip: Recruit as many lenders as possible. Keep a shortlist of the most reliable lenders. This is the list that you will go to first!

Private Money Lender

You have 3 reliable private lenders that offer you attractive interest rates. With this leverage, you could lend out money at a higher interest rate to make a profit. They all lend at a 5% interest rate. You offer loans to potential clients at a 10% interest rate. Two rehabbers need $800,000 for two different San Francisco rehab projects and another rehabber needs $500,000 for a Manhattan project.

10% of $800,000 = $80,000

10% of $800,000 = $80,000

10% of $500,000 = $50,000

Gross total = $210,000 – $105,000 (your debt to lenders) =

Net total = $105,000 (your profit)

Tip: Recruit as many lenders as possible. Keep a shortlist of the most reliable lenders. This is the list that you will go to first!

Tax lien investor

You have realized that investing your money in CDs and money market accounts are not going to make you wealthy. You're still skeptical about the stock market and find that bonds are not much better than CDs. Real estate has historically been one of the more stable investments. However, you prefer a "hands off" approach to real estate investing. So, you decide to invest in tax liens. You want to make $100,000 in a 1 year. So, you decide to invest a state with a high interest rate. You choose Illinois.

Illinois property: $214,000 (fair market value)
                        $3,940 (tax lien value)

You buy the tax lien for $3,940. You are excited about the 18% interest rate and look forward to cash out. However, the homeowner doesn't redeem the property, which means you become the owner of the property. The house is "free and clear" but needs a lot of work. You don't want to deal with the headache and prefer a quick sale. You decide to sell it for half of the fair market value and now have several interested buyers. You sell it to the first buyer with cash and walk away with $107,000.

Tip: If you want the best chances of redeeming the property using little money, consider investing in tax deeds, redeemable deeds, or "subject to" properties. While you may be able to redeem a property from a tax lien, investors mainly buy tax liens because of the high interest rates!

So, whichever real estate method that you employ, you can make a 6 figure salary if you are REALLY <u>determined</u>. No excuses!

CHAPTER 12

At The Crossroads

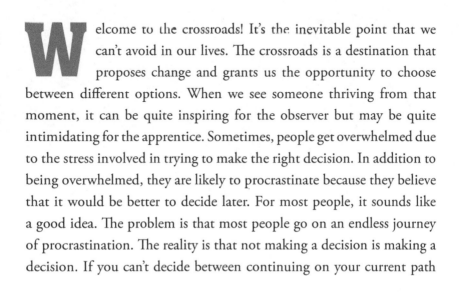

Welcome to the crossroads! It's the inevitable point that we can't avoid in our lives. The crossroads is a destination that proposes change and grants us the opportunity to choose between different options. When we see someone thriving from that moment, it can be quite inspiring for the observer but may be quite intimidating for the apprentice. Sometimes, people get overwhelmed due to the stress involved in trying to make the right decision. In addition to being overwhelmed, they are likely to procrastinate because they believe that it would be better to decide later. For most people, it sounds like a good idea. The problem is that most people go on an endless journey of procrastination. The reality is that not making a decision is making a decision. If you can't decide between continuing on your current path or starting on a new one, then you have already decided to continue on your current path. One good analogy is the train ride. You are riding on a train that has multiple stops between Los Angeles and Orlando. During the train ride, you can either get off at the next stop or continue to ride the train. If you are unable to come to a decision at the arrival of each stop, you will continue to ride the train by default.

Most people who choose by default are not usually happy with their decisions but they have learned to live with them anyway. Mediocrity is not a foreign principle in our society. While our society encourages success, it also encourages mediocrity. It is a state that most humans accept as the norm, despite being deprived of their true desires. The major aspects of life (career, family, friends, love, etc) for an average Joe is decided by happenstance and not consciously. It is only by making conscious changes that people will see significant changes in their quality of life. So, why do people resort to choosing by default rather than choosing consciously? People choose by default because they lack clarity.

How can a person establish clarity at the crossroads? There are multiple ways that a person can establish clarity but I will name a few here. One way is by a person creating a "pros and cons" list regarding their choices. After they have created the list, they should be able to make a choice based on the things they value the most. Another way is choosing the path with the most potential and the least risk. However, we are not always presented with such choices. Often, the crossroads present a "safe" path and a "risky" path. If the risky path offers at least a minimum standard of living as the worst case scenario, the risky path should be strongly considered. When we choose the safe path, we often find ourselves regretting not taking the more challenging path. Another way that happens to be one of my favorites is having a mentor. There is not a better way to guarantee success. A mentor has already faced your challenges and can provide guidance to help you overcome the anticipated obstacles. It has been proven that you're much more likely to be successful with a mentor than without one. A study conducted by the American Society for Training and Development found that 75% of executives attribute their success to having a mentor. It's important to remember that a mentor isn't meant to be your parent, friend, or even a generous investor. A mentor is a business veteran whose role is to tell what you really need to hear about your career path. They can be your cheerleader at times but their real value is in their objective, unvarnished advice.

So, how does a person find the right mentor? Dr. Michael Woodward (or better known as Dr. Woody) advises that a person should find someone whose past experiences align with their future ambitions. He further advises that it's important to feel comfortable with your mentor because the relationship has to be open and honest in order for it to be effective. As in any relationship, chemistry is important. Before you start looking for mentors, take some time to determine exactly what qualities that you are looking for in a mentor. This step will save you a lot of time and bring you much closer to finding a compatible mentor. I would start by searching for people you already know since you will likely be more comfortable with them. What if you're unable to find a suitable match based on the people that you already know? Then, it's time that you put yourself out there. Attend meetings at your local chamber of commerce and other local business groups, alumni networking and charity events, and events sponsored by national groups. Be sure to meet as many people as you can because the more people that you meet, the more likely you are to find the perfect mentor for you.

There are 2 good resources that can help you find a mentor: MicroMentor and SCORE. MicroMentor is a free service that connects entrepreneurs with volunteer mentors to solve problems and build businesses together. Every mentor brings a unique set of experiences to the MicroMentor community. They range in occupation and industry, from successful small business owners to active CFOs and middle managers at large companies. Whether entrepreneurs need help with business planning, market strategy, finance, or some other area, you can find a match on MicroMentor. Their website is www.micromentor.org. SCORE (also known as Service Corps Of Retired Executives) is another free service that offers articles, online workshops, and the ability to connect with SCORE experts to answer your business related questions online or in person. Their website is www.score.org.

One common question that I'm asked regarding mentorships is: "Why would a mentor want to help me?" Surprisingly, mentors are happy to work with business owners, entrepreneurs, and work professionals because someone once helped them and they want to return the favor. Please keep in mind that mentors are busy with other things (like their career, family, etc), so always come prepared to avoid wasting their time. Some mentors will charge for their time to hold mentees accountable and as a measure to assure that their time is being valued. As Americans, most of us take a lot of the free stuff for granted. A person may see something like SCORE or MicroMentor and will be excited about the level and quality of service. The problem is that they won't finish with the mentorship or will never get started with a mentor. If someone that you respect highly is offering a mentorship for a fee, I would highly recommend it. It is from someone that you respect greatly and you will take it more seriously since you are paying for it.

If you are at the crossroads, you are at a point where you must make a decision that will likely affect your life in the next several years. Let's say that chapter 3 or 4 applies to you. You've wanted to get out of that crazy work schedule at McDonald's and now you have the chance. You got a job offer in the Bakken area in North Dakota that pays a salary of $45,000/year. There is a part of you that is scared because this move will take you out of your comfort zone, despite how much you hate it. It's normal for anyone to be nervous about entering into a new chapter of their life. However, if you are living paycheck to paycheck making $9/hr and financial security really matters to you, then it may be much easier for you to make the transition. Let's say that chapter 5 or 6 applies to you. You just graduated out of high school and would love to go to college but you're worried about the high costs of tuition and the 4 year investment. You are aware of the "credit by examination" option and the "scholarship" option. You're not sure about the best route for you. You could go to college for free on a scholarship and do the 4 years. Or you could go the "credit by examination" route and finish in 1 year. Which is the best option for you? The true answer is only you will know what's ultimately right for you.

Let's say that chapter 7 or 8 applies to you. You are tired of your current career and desire for something new. You don't really want to go back to school and prefer something that is somewhat related to your new desired career. If you are thinking of going into the non-profit world, you should have little to no challenges in making the transition. What if you are not considering in going into the non-profit world? One of the fears that I hear from people is "I probably won't be that successful in my new career if I don't go back to school." It is true that there are some careers that you definitely need a degree and prior work experience since those careers are specialized. Be proactive though. See if there are relevant positions within your company and ask your boss if it's possible to transition into one of those careers. If your current company doesn't offer what you're seeking, consider doing an internship. All employers don't require interns to have an educational background that is relevant to their internship. So, ask around and see if an internship is a possibility with your qualifications. There is no reason why someone should be limited to the option of going back to school to start a new career. You have options! Now, go ahead and make use of them!

I could go on and talk about possible scenarios that are unique to each chapter. The particular chapter is not important because being at the crossroads prompts you all to do one thing: DECIDE. Figure out what are the 3 most important things in your life and based your decision on those things. So, what is your decision? Remember, if you don't make a decision, then you have made your decision.

CHAPTER 13

Almost There

You are almost there! At this point, you're probably about two-thirds of the way there. If you haven't faced any adversity yet, it doesn't mean that it isn't coming. Sometimes, adversity arrives towards the end. Adversity is tricky because you can't predict the arrival nor the amount of it when it arrives to you. In any venture, you will need a good offense and defense if you plan on being successful. Adversity is and will always be your opponent. The level of your confidence will ultimately determine whether you'll be successful or not. Good sports teams don't always thrive because of their great talent. They thrive because of their high level of confidence. Being talented isn't always a factor. Mediocre sports teams have made it to the playoffs because their confidence was the main driver. If you plan on beating adversity, you must be and remain confident.

Adversity arrives as a result of your ignorance, mistakes, or lack of confidence. It is impossible to avoid adversity. In any new venture, making mistakes is just as certain as dying. You need to remember that mistakes are part of the learning process. Even the most successful people have risen from their mistakes. When you are not scared of making mistakes, you become fearless in taking risks and wiser from every experience. Confidence is a necessary trait in any pursuit. If you are not confident in yourself, then you need to learn to be more confident. Reflect back on your past successes and use those experiences as your foundation. Henry Ford said it best: "Whether you think you can or think you can't, either way you're right." It's the mind that makes it so. When you are confident in yourself, you influence others to be confident in you. When others are confident in you, you become more confident in yourself and this cycle repeats itself indefinitely.

In chapter 1, I talked about the differences between a motive and motivation. Motive is the specific reason for performing a specific action. An example of a motive is the following: "*I want to be self-employed because I prefer to create my own schedule and make my own decisions.*" Motivation is the feeling that makes you want to perform the specific action. An example of motivation is the following: "*I do not like working long hours and working on the weekends.*" So, do you remember what your motive is? What about your motivation? The last component to the equation is confidence. It will be very difficult to be successful by having the first two components and not having the last one. So, what is "motive + motivation – confidence"? Procrastination (as discussed in chapter 2)! Having passionate thoughts without taking action is procrastination. Procrastination is dangerous. In fact, it is just as dangerous as crossing the street without looking both ways. The only difference is that the pain is interpreted differently. Getting hit by a vehicle is very likely to cause a person some form of physical injury, while procrastination is very likely to result in some form of emotional suffering in a person. The most common procrastination alibi is "I'll do it later." People don't realize that procrastination labels the word "later" as indefinite. It can be a bad habit to develop because it gives room for distractions, which usually makes people forget about their initial goals.

This pain can start compounding if a person continues to ignore their goals. The truth of the matter is that your age is never a factor because you can always make that choice to move forward. You are welcome to allow old age to hinder you but it didn't hinder Colonel Sanders. Colonel Sanders is a great example of consistent confidence. He was 65 years old before KFC became profitable. Before he became recognized as "Colonel Sanders", Harland was a sixth grade dropout and an unsuccessful political candidate. Prior to his success, he served in multiple professions. He was a farmhand, railroad worker, insurance salesman, gas station operator, and a tire salesman. He certainly wasn't dealt a good hand of cards. At the age of 6, his father died which forced his mother to enter the workforce to support the family. At the age of 40, he started selling fried chicken from his Kentucky roadside restaurant in the Great Depression.

The Great Depression was quite an adversary to most Americans during that time. The nation's unemployment rate rose over 60% in 3 years, giving the U.S. a 25% unemployment rate. Farming and rural areas suffered as crop prices fell by 60%. Industrial production was down by 46% and foreign trade down by 70%. Businesses and families defaulted on record numbers of loans and more than 5,000 banks had failed. Almost a half million of Americans was homeless and began congregating in shanty towns – communities usually found in third world countries. Again, life during the Great Depression was quite challenging even for Harland Sanders.

Nine years later, he acquired a motel in Asheville, North Carolina. About two months later, his Kentucky restaurant was destroyed in a fire but Sanders decided to rebuild it as a motel with a 140 seat restaurant. As the U.S. entered World War II in 1941, gas was rationed and Sanders was forced to close his Asheville motel. Eleven years later, he franchised "Kentucky Fried Chicken" for the first time to Pete Harman, who owned one of South Salt Lake's largest restaurants. Sanders' fried chicken stood out from the competitors since it was a product from Kentucky and evoked Southern hospitality, which is uncommon in Utah. At the age of 65, Colonel Sanders had the first fast food chain to expand internationally. About ten years later with 600+ franchised restaurants, he sold Kentucky Fried Chicken (U.S.) for $2 million to a group of investors and stayed with the company as a salaried brand ambassador.

Colonel Sanders faced tremendous adversity but he persisted with consistent confidence. Does adversity frighten you? It didn't frighten Colonel Sanders. After all, he said "Every failure is a stepping stone to something better. I was rejected 1,009 times before selling my first franchise and then my company for $2 million. So, many other people have strived through adversity that it will embarrass you." If Colonel Sanders' persistence was a result of his success, what's stopping you from persisting? I have always said that every time that you fail, it means that you're getting closer to success. This statement may not sit well with a lot of people but it is the truth indeed. Success is the result of failure acceptance and continued persistence.

Do you quit dating because a few people told you that they weren't interested?

Do you quit working because a few employers told that you weren't a good fit?

Do you quit applying for certain positions because a few employers implied that females don't succeed in that industry?

Do you quit your new business venture because your friends tell you that most businesses fail in the first 5 years?

If you have answered YES to any of those questions, please return to chapter 1. If you have answered NO to all of those questions, you have all that you need to be a success. If you ever need any encouragement, keep the following facts in mind.

Abraham Lincoln suffered a series of lost elections before he went to become one of the greatest presidents.

Michael Jordan was cut from the high school basketball team before he went to play for UNC and then the Chicago Bulls.

J.K. Rowling was a divorced, single mother who struggled by living on welfare before her profitable Harry Potter brand, which was initially rejected by 12 publishers.

In order to overcome adversity, you need a good offense and defense. Think of a chess game. If you're aggressive in your approach, you are likely to have a poor defense. If you're passive in your approach, you are likely to have a poor offense. Incorporating a good balance will provide a good offense and defense. Also, consider bringing competent members onto your team. Recruit people that possess strengths in areas that are your weaknesses. In most ventures, it is better to work as a team rather than working alone. Almost every successful business has become successful because they initially had a team. The size of the team is not really important. It's more about your team members' experience, education, and aptitude. Facing adversity as a team is much easier to overcome than facing it alone. Adversity may be your opponent but it is also a good teacher. Keep pressing on!

CHAPTER 14

Reaching The Finish Line

Congratulations! You have reached THE FINISH LINE. How do you feel? Fulfilled? Satisfied? Excited? Surely, it is one of those emotions, if not them all. What is it all worth it? Of course it is. After all, if it wasn't worth it, you probably would have given up a long time ago. We all wish to be successful but few actually want to be successful. I am so happy for you. Before you thank me, I would thank yourself first because your only obstacle with anything is yourself. Therefore, you are the primary factor of your success.

"Success is the best revenge." This is an old adage that has existed for decades but more importantly it's a subjective statement. If you feel that this statement fits the bill, then you're just as right as someone who disagrees with you. However, if you are obsessed in resulting to revenge, then you should do it through success. Revenge can be illustrated in different ways. A person may take revenge for being dumped by a significant other for an illegitimate reason. Or a person may take revenge for being overlooked on a job promotion. Another reason can be attributed to someone's incompetence for a career, even if it is due to a disability. It is against the law for employers to be discriminative in this way but most applicants fail to take any action in fighting this injustice. While the "revenge" mindset may not be healthy, it can very likely bring more success in your life. Disabled people are one of the most common examples of people who are often doubted of being successful.

Very Successful People Who Were Disabled Prior To The Fame

Stephen Hawking is one of the most well-known physicists in the world and he was able to achieve it despite being diagnosed with at the age of 21.

DJ Paul is a respected and well-known urban musician and part of the success of 2 of their platinum albums. He is known most for his production talents, despite having a crippled arm. He won an Academy Award with bandmate, Juicy J, for "Best Original Song."

Marlee Matlin, an Academy Award actress, is one of the most successful deaf actresses. She was deaf ever since she was 18 months old.

Franklin D. Roosevelt has been recognized for being one of our greatest presidents, despite being confined to a wheelchair due to having polio.

Helen Keller was the first deaf and blind person to earn a college degree. She is known worldwide for her 12 published books, including the spiritual autobiography, My Religion.

Perhaps, success is the best revenge for some people.

Well, you have achieved your goal. So, what's the next step? Only you will know. You may choose to expand your goal into something bigger. For example, perhaps your goal was to secure a career in human resources. You can expand that goal by creating a temporary staffing agency once you feel obtained enough experience in your HR career. Another option in taking the next step is choosing to pursue something different entirely. You have proven to yourself that success is only achieved when a person doesn't allow themselves to be the obstacle.

Please visit reachingthefinishline.com to share your success stories and stay informed on upcoming events.

CHAPTER 15

More Options To Consider

The information provided in the previous chapters is sufficient for anyone ready to get started. In addition to that information, I will provide supplemental resources in this chapter to help readers wanting to get on the fast track. While it is not necessary to your success, I would definitely recommend them to shorten your learning curve and bring you to success faster.

From the introduction to chapter 2 and from chapter 13 to 15, I talk about the mindset required for readers to be successful in anything. Procrastination is the main factor that cripples people from moving forward. Joseph Ferrari, a leading international researcher in the study of procrastination, has found that 20% of Americans are chronic procrastinators. When you consider the population of our nation, 20%

is a high figure. That's higher than the number of people diagnosed with clinical depression or phobias. Procrastination is significantly higher among college students, which is also linked to lower salaries and higher likelihood of unemployment. They can waste up to a third of their time with distractions like sleeping, watching television, or playing video games. We have such an abundance of procrastinators that our society accommodates it. One example is filing yearly tax returns. Most U.S. post offices stay open later on April 15th which in effect accommodates procrastination. How about providing incentives for taxpayers who file early? In that case, the government doesn't become the victim of procrastination and the taxpayer gets rewarded for filing early. Another example is Christmas shopping. Various retailers extend their business hours during the Christmas holiday to accommodate procrastinators. I think we all can agree that it's harder to abstain from procrastination when society encourages it.

Next year, I will be offering motivational seminars to my followers. These seminars will not be anything like the common ones. I want my followers to be successful. In order to enhance the success of my followers, I will be holding all of my followers accountable. My accountability program's format is ALL or NOTHING. It's for people who are REALLY SERIOUS about achieving success.

In chapters 3 and 4, I talk about how to land a great career without having a high school diploma or college degree. Most of our parents have indoctrinated us to get our diploma and/or degree because they think success cannot be achieved without it. Penelope Trunk, founder of Brazen Careerist, says that college does not provide any significant leadership or managerial skill development. In 2013, 35% of high school graduates did not enroll in college after graduating from high school, the highest figure in the last two decades. She advises that the best path to a great career is by doing several internships. I'm not suggesting for teenagers and young adults to drop out school. Nevertheless, I think it's important for an individual to evaluate their situation and make an educated decision based on their available options.

Next year, I will be offering career seminars to my followers. Several representatives from various employers will be present to talk to you more about their companies and career opportunities. I'm planning for it to be a 2 day seminar. The first day will be dedicated to preparation (i.e. creating an attractive resume, acing an interview, etc). The second day will be dedicated to job placement (i.e. learning about several companies and their career opportunities, conducting interviews with qualified attendees, etc). My intent is for my followers to be better prepared professionally and secure a great career. At the end of the 2 day seminar, most attendees will receive interviews and/or a job offer.

In chapter 5, I talk about how to go to college for free. Most people do not have the money to afford a college education. There are also a lot of people that are wary in paying for college because they are not sure if it'll be worth the investment. The chapter provides multiple tuition-free options. If you are flexible about the college location, there are a variety of options that might be a good fit for you. If you experienced an unfortunate situation like unemployment, a victim of 9/11 or a natural disaster, there are options available for you. If you are a Medicaid recipient, veteran, state employee, or an employee of select universities, there are options available for you too. What's better than getting a college education without having to pay for it? Next year, I will be offering educational seminars about increasing your chances in securing tuition-free education. Several graduates of these scholarship programs will be present to talk to you about how to dramatically increase your chances in getting a scholarship award.

In chapter 6, I talk about how to graduate with a bachelor's degree in 1 year. 60% of students take more than 4 years to graduate with a bachelor's degree, according to the Department of Education. The main reason for the delay is that students have difficulty balancing work and school. Most students take jobs to compensate for the lack of student aid or financial support provided by their parents. A lot of students are unaware of credit by examination providers, which can allow a student to save enormous amounts of money and graduate in 1 year. Wouldn't you rather condense the 4 years of college into 1 year? Next year, I will be offering educational seminars regarding the alternative path to a college education through credit by examination providers. While a college degree is not required to be successful in any career, my intent is for the seminar to provide more clarity about the available options.

In chapter 7, I talk about how to change careers without going back to college. There are 2 types of profiles that describe a person who is facing this challenge. One type is a person who spent a few years in their initial career but no longer interested in continuing it. There are several reasons why people lose interest in their careers but I will discuss the 3 common reasons. One reason is that changes in a person's personal life. People are likely to change the careers when more family time or a higher income is the priority. Another reason is a natural loss of interest. Some people may start in a career that they love only to realize later that it is no longer fulfilling. Another reason that encourages people to lose interest is career burnout. Some people get stuck in careers where they have to work 55+ hour weeks. The burnout becomes overwhelming because it starts affecting a person's mental and physical health. The other type is a student who gets toward the end of their college education to only realize that they are no longer interested in their major. Carnegie Mellon University discovered that one of the reasons is due to prior discouraging experiences from similar courses. Another common reason is students naturally lose interest because they find other career fields that are more interesting and exciting.

Next year, I will be offering career change seminars to my followers. Several representatives from for-profit corporations and non-profit organizations (as discussed in chapter 8) will be present to talk to you more about their companies, career opportunities, and how your qualifications can be a good fit for some of their available positions. At the end of the seminar, most attendees will receive interviews and/or job offers.

In chapters 9 and 10, I talk about how to make a full-time income in unconventional ways. Usually, most people get paid hourly on a 5 to 6 day work week or are salaried employees on a 40+ hour work week. However, there are careers that allow a person to work from home full-time or work a schedule that gives a person the opportunity to travel and have 3 to 4 months off a year. The thing that people really want is flexibility. One of the most effective ways to have happy and hardworking employees is to allow them to make reasonable adjustments to their schedules, which will bring the most efficiency in both work and their personal lives. Almost 80% of U.S. workers want to work from home at least part-time, according to Global Workplace Analytics. Companies that provide flexible work options can reduce employee turnover. It is estimated that over $11 billion is lost annually due to employee turnover, according to The Bureau of National Affairs.

Next year, I will be offering career seminars to my followers. Several representatives from various employers will be present to talk to you more about their companies, career opportunities, and flexible work options. At the end of your seminar, you will have more clarity on your options and may even go home with a job!

In chapter 11, I talk about how to make a 6 figure salary without having a license or prior experience. For some reason, a lot of people think that real estate is limited to contractors, brokers, realtors, and property managers. The real reason is that they are ignorant about the other professions in the industry. There are several real estate niches for novices to take in consideration. Some niches are better options for some people than others. However, there is no reason why you can't be successful in any one of them. The only thing that can get in your way is

YOU. Next year, I will be offering real estate seminars to my followers. Each real estate seminar will be unique because it will focus on 1 real estate niche. These seminars are perfect for the person who wants to get started immediately and go for the fast track to success.

In regards to all of my seminars, some of them will be free and others will be priced affordably. These seminars can be a great supplement to your college education or even replace it (if you have never attended). Most people have no problem paying for a college education. That's a good and a bad thing. I think it's a good thing because a person paying for education shows their commitment in learning. However, I think it's bad when people pay insane amounts of money for education that can be offered at a cheaper price elsewhere. No one should be deprived of getting an education because of expensive tuition costs. I can assure you that all of my offerings will be free or no more than the average cost of a community college course. Go to reachingthefinishline.com to stay tuned.

About the Author

Kallen Diggs is a real estate expert, personal development coach, public speaker, and career consultant. Kallen has helped hundreds of people overcome their fears and live up to their full potential. He is a member of the National Association of Independent Writers and Editors and has articles published by the Genesis Communications Network, which hosts radio shows of Kate Delaney (Emmy award winner), Stephen Baldwin (Hollywood icon & reality TV star), and Dani Johnson (ABC's Secret Millionaire).

Kallen is the owner and CEO of Wholesome Homes, a Michigan based real estate company. He lives in Austin, Texas and enjoys hiking, watching documentaries, and traveling abroad.

Printed in the USA
CPSIA information can be obtained
at www.ICGtesting.com
JSHW022329140824
68134JS00019B/1371